— The —
Reluctant Immigrant

A Memoir

Mary Neville

Copyright © 2015 Mary Neville
All rights reserved
First Edition

PAGE PUBLISHING, INC.
New York, NY

First originally published by Page Publishing, Inc. 2015

ISBN 978-1-63417-762-7 (pbk)
ISBN 978-1-63417-763-4 (digital)
ISBN 978-1-68139-331-5 (hardcover)

Printed in the United States of America

CHAPTER ONE

The Citie of London that is so Dere

> "The citie of London that is so dere to me,
> So dere and sweete, on which I was forth
> growen; and more kindly love hath I to
> that place than to any other in yerth."
>
> — Geofrey Chaucer
> born on Thames Street near the Tower of
> London 1343–1400

In the early morning light of May 20, 1968, I stood bewildered and confused on the bustling quay with my fellow passengers as I watched them disembark from our luxury ship that had been our home for the last five days, the large French liner, *The France*. Some of the departing passengers were searching for faces they might know among the throng of people who were meeting the ship, and others seemed to be arriving at their home port destination, happy and comfortable in their arrival. But I, however, recognized nothing in the daunting cityscape. What I did feel was part apprehension and part curiosity as I watched the great crowd of people gradually disperse, some moving away from the quay into waiting cars and buses, while others wandered away on foot, soon to be swallowed up and incorporated into the bustling population of New York City.

I stood with my little family far apart from the crowd, in the hope that we would be more easily spotted by the driver sent from the large American corporation that had brought us from England and where Richard would soon be working. He would be joining what had been described in the sixties as an exodus of very smart scientists and other highly qualified people, mostly men, referred to as the European Brain Drain. It was at this crucial moment as my eyes scanned the busy, changing scene of the crowd as it slowly moved away from the dock, spreading out and then becoming lost in the city streets, that I saw a man with a gun in his hip holster standing quite close to us. Horrified and alarmed, I instinctively moved as far away as I could from the man and gathered the children to my side, shielding them from potential danger, trying to alert Richard's attention at the same time. As I focused more closely, I noticed that the paunchy, middle-aged man with the gun was also wearing a rather rumpled uniform, his hat pushed back off his forehead, which was sweating profusely from the scorching high heat of the day, and he was chewing gum. One hand seemed to be affectionately hovering close to the gun, which was attached to his belt and slung low under his protruding belly. Having never, ever seen a gun before in my entire life, the look of grave consternation on my face must have been obvious to him, and at that moment, I caught his eye just as he gave me a broad, semi-reassuring smile and a wrinkled wink. Embarrassed, I couldn't help concealing a small smile myself as I felt my tension ease slightly, but only slightly, I was shocked by what I had seen. I then supposed and hoped that he might just be a New York policeman on duty and while still concerned and not at all reassured about the gun and why he would need it, I lowered my eyes, hoping he would go farther away and lose himself in the crowd. When I looked up a few minutes later he had gone, but I was amused by this "keystone cop" and his out-of-shape` appearance and couldn't imagine him in hot pursuit of a suspect, which made me think that discharging a bullet to stop a culprit would be easier than chasing and tackling and that using a weapon might be a common practice in this country and I felt the wave of anxiety return.

For a minute I remembered affectionately the dignified demeanor and bristling smart turnout of the London policeman and missed their efficient courtesy and the fact that none of the police force in England carried a firearm. Comforted for a minute, I swiveled my head around to take in more of the busy scene, my neck aching slightly as I looked up to see the tall skyscrapers but they seemed to be leaning too close for a comfortable view, causing me to feel dizzy and claustrophobic. The sky scrapers of New York seemed to be falling on top of me and the noise and giddy, excited chaos was beginning to make me feel faint. Was I ready for this enormous change? I realized that so many things were going to be strange and different, challenging and perhaps even hostile here. I struggled to control my acute apprehension and my tears. I felt as though I had been coerced into this enormous life-changing decision and felt resentful. How would I cope?

At last the driver of the car arrived and ushered us into the huge, long vehicle, in fact it was a limousine, which was needed to transport us and all of our worldly goods on the journey to the first of our many addresses in America. The children squealed and giggled as they clambered into the vast space. "We could get our whole Mini inside this big car." My four-year-old Beth laughed, delighted with the newness and strangeness of her surroundings. Apart from the many cases we had also brought two trunks with us. Clothes and personal items were in most of the cases, but the trunks contained all the books and long playing classical records we were so attached to that we couldn't bear to leave them behind.

The drive to Media, Pennsylvania, and our first home seemed endless. The highways system was overwhelming. I had never seen so many car lanes loaded with so much traffic, and the large fast cars would fly passed us furiously as if in hot pursuit of something vital. The cars themselves were enormous compared to English cars, which reminded me more of dinky toy cars in comparison. We were now in the state of New Jersey, which called itself "The Garden State," but my heart sank when we drove past a place called Elizabeth. I grimaced in horror at the sight. As far as my eye could see, there were acres of oil refineries and tall suspicious chimneys belching out what appeared to be very noxious smoke, and the whole place looked like a sinister wasteland. "I thought New Jersey was called the Garden State," I groaned in Richard's ear. "It's a vast state so don't judge it too soon. This is just its industrial part, but believe me, it is full of rich agricultural land and beautiful beaches that you will love," he reassured, asserting his new knowledge. I wondered who the poor woman Elizabeth was, whose name had been so unkindly used. I realized I had not been adequately equipped on the geography of this, our new home, and had better brush up and catch up quickly.

I dozed sullenly, not able to digest any more new information that day. My emotions swirled around in my brain. On the one hand I needed to be positive as much for the children's sake as for my own, but I still ached from an uneasy, gnawing sensation, recognizing that at this moment I was definitely a foot-dragging and very reluctant new immigrant to these United States. I just wanted to go home to my family and to London where I was born and brought up.

French Line - SS France

A grand view of the SS France
Author's private collection

Still fresh in my mind was the Statue of Liberty incident. Richard had woken all of us at four that morning in the last few remaining hours of our journey across the Atlantic before we docked in New York harbor. With a wake-up call sounding so alarming I thought the ship was about to sink, Richard was urging us all to hurry and quickly get dressed so we could dash up on deck in the cold damp of early dawn to watch as we sailed passed the Statue of Liberty. Grumbling loudly I shook the children hurriedly out of their slumber, threw clothes on them, and raced through the ship to find that there were only a handful of people on the deck for the event because most of the sensible passengers were still asleep, cozy in their cabins, but my inner protest became aroused because while I respected the history of the country and what the statues had represented, neither I nor my family fitted the description of one of the huddled masses yearning to be free. This was at the crux of my disenchantment with this experiment. The days of sailing across the great Atlantic should have been a wonderful experience, but as I walked the decks dispiritedly, the cool ocean spray washing away my salty tears as I only pretended to embrace the adventure. I had not wanted to leave England.

The family farewell scene at the station in London was almost unbearable. My mother was too upset and gripped with sadness to see us leave; it was far too painful for her to say good-bye. It was hard enough to see me, her eldest and closest daughter leave, but to be parted from three-year-old Beth and one-year-old Andrew both of whom she adored passionately was, to her, unthinkable. A close, normal relationship with her two beloved grandchildren would be impossible now and it almost broke her heart knowing she would not be able to watch them develop through their various stages of growth and enjoy the close connection she wanted to have with them and that they needed to have with her. Sadly none of that would be possible now. Her anguish had made her ill, so it was up to my father to carry out the difficult task and to be the strong parent who would wave us off on the boat train from London's Waterloo station. He was very brave, and coming from a family of actors, he put on a clown's cheerful smile and wore a cloak of bravado, but it was torture for him too because we were also very close and he, like my mother, adored his two young grandchildren, and he had also looked forward to years of the usual grand- parenting joys. At first my father kept up briskly with the train waving furiously, his trilby hat in his hand like a flag as the long boat train strained to pull its huge weight and slowly move it along the platform. Then he had to start running as it increased its speed toward the wide curve, which took it out of the station. My head was hanging out of the window, waving madly, trying to catch the last glimpse of my darling father. Then he just stopped, still, motionless, except for his face which collapsed into tears, and then his shoulders shuddered with silent sobs and the rest of his body crumpled before me as he disappeared from my view.

I closed my eyes and began to reminisce, seeing vividly in my mind the life I had left behind. I was already missing my home, my family, and my friends in London's south east district and was proud to have been born in that great city's historic and beautiful Royal Borough of Greenwich and, as it happened, in the middle of a German air raid in March of 1940. Greenwich had the great river Thames running through it and the enemy found the river a very appealing target for most of the war. I was also very proud of my brave parents as they comforted and reassured me through countless terrifying nights, many spent in the dark, dampness of the Anderson shelter built by the London County Council for Londoners who were living within the "danger zone." The shelter was erected in the garden as far away from the house structure as was feasibly possible. They were safe and probably saved thousands of lives, and erected a number of feet deep into the ground, they seemed sturdy but also crudely constructed from tin metal sheeting so they gave little comfort, except for the comfort that came from the small level of reassurance they provided. They had to have two feet of soil on top of the tin roof probably to conceal them from enemy aircraft but also to be utilized for the growing of some flowers and vegetables. All Londoner's in the city were provided with gas masks, and I, like all the children, regardless of age carried their Mickey Mouse gas masks everywhere, to be safe—just in case. Sometimes if a raid was expected we squeezed together like sardines in a little cupboard under the staircase of our house, because if a house was hit the stairwell usually survived the blast and offered vulnerable Londoners some small protection. If my mother was alone with me and only a little scared, or wasn't sure an attack would be close, we got under the dining room table which, of course, would have offered little protection if the house had been hit and collapsed on top of us. But it offered some small reassurance, and psychologically that helped, because most of the time there was an overwhelming feeling among Londoners of complete and absolute exhaustion, caused by living in an almost-permanent state of fear. I was deeply loved and bravely cared for during those days and nights of bewildering terror. Londoners everywhere came together in their shared sacrifice and hardship during that awful testing time of the Blitz, which included seventy-six consecutive nights of bombing when forty-thousand civilians were killed. Those who had survived the Blitz were utterly war weary as they struggled for another four years only to be visited by the enemies' last cruel gasp when they confronted London and other big cities in 1944 with the first of the deadly rockets, the V-I and later, even worse the V-II that came murderously out of the silent sky and fell indiscriminately on the civilians. There was almost no warning to scramble for shelter. Deeply scarred and with the city almost unrecognizable from the constant bombing, Londoners did eventually recover and could hold heads high with pride for the many sacrifices made by all and for the endurance and bloody-minded determination to beat the odds set against them. During London's long and great history, the people had always been tested and had come through over and over again, with their strength, humor, determination, and stoicism. I was very proud of that courageous heritage.

I loved London with a passion and I watched her heal and grow, as I clipped along her streets, aware of her like a big sister by my side, growing, healing, and gaining strength again after the war, just as I was also growing and becoming stronger year after year. The city was my playground and offered an ever-changing backdrop of sumptuous feasts waiting for me to explore. Music, art, theatre, architecture, parks, and a myriad of centuries-old winding streets and alleyways were all around me, and I could hear the echo of the city's history marching in time with me.

The pleasure in finding out the deeper history of the neighborhood in which I was born and brought up has been thrilling, although much of what I have rediscovered had been mulling around in my memory from experience and history lessons taught long ago. In 1997, Greenwich was honored by UNESCO as a World Heritage Centre "for the concentration of the building and quality of buildings of historic and architectural interest." It also tells us from their historical research that the area has been "favored by humankind since the Bronze Age, as demonstrated by the burial mounds and a large first to fourth century AD Roman villa that have been discovered in Greenwich Park." The royal park itself "was laid out in the 1660s and reflects two centuries of growth and development in the area that was Greenwich and is considered a masterpiece of the application of symmetrical landscape design to an irregular terrain." This whole area including its neighbor, Blackheath in the south was closer to where I lived and played, and was my local neighborhood, and from a young age, I was taken regularly to the old Royal Park by my parents for fun and recreation. The park was a lovely place for picnics beside the glorious flower beds—horticulture being every Englishman's passion—and I remember running wild through its luscious green and wooded parkland and frolicking in its long grasses and natural spaces, home to towering, broad and majestic trees of every variety, many of them planted at the beginning of the park's development, making them hundreds of years old. "Greenwich Royal Park is a formal plan, arranged symmetrically on either side of is main north-south axis, which is aligned on the beautiful 17th century Queen's House built by Inigo Jones that sits alongside the River Thames." From the flat but higher end of the park, the land falls away steeply creating an irresistible place for centuries of children to run until they rolled to a stop. The view from the top of the park is spectacular, with the beautiful river and the elegant buildings alongside the embankment all seeming to shine below in whatever the weather. Those buildings symmetrically arranged on either side of Queen's House are part of an array of other masterpieces by Sir Christopher Wren and include his palatial master plan complex of the Royal Hospital and the Royal Navel College and the Greenwich Royal Park surrounds all of them like a green, jeweled necklace.

If you approach the park from Blackheath, which was closer to my home and keep walking through the tall wrought-iron gates on to the main path, you eventually come to the wide, steep space that takes you down to the river. "In 1675 Christopher Wren and the scientist Robert Hooke designed and built the turreted, red brick octagonal building on the bluff of Greenwich Hill, the Royal Observatory, overlooking the old palace for John Flamsteed, the first English Astronomer Royal. Greenwich established its pre-eminence in this field and it was here in 1884 that the Greenwich Meridian and Greenwich Mean Time were adopted as world standards for the measurements of space and time." The area around Maritime Greenwich is a UNESCO World Heritage Centre.

The heath itself is one of the largest areas of common land in Greater London and its name is recorded in 1166 as Blachehedfeld, which means "dark-colored heathland." It has been a well- known rallying point for a variety of causes through the centuries. There is a road in the area named after the popular peasant leader Wat Tyler who led the Peasants' Revolt on the heath in 1381, followed by the Jack Cades Kentish rebellion there in 1450. From the west of England came the Cornish rebels who were defeated at the Battle of Blackheath in 1497. The list is long and mostly gory. In the seventeenth and eighteenth centuries, it was a notorious haunt of highwaymen because the main road from London to the south coast went through Blackheath, so there were "easy pickings." The other unresolved question is whether the heath was used to bury some of the victims of the Black Death or Plague in 1665 and that is still an on-going discussion. All I know is how I loved the place, the small quaint village down the steep hill from the heath, which still holds onto its charming features today–the heathland seemed to me to be set high and free, its location marked by a pretty church built in 1830, which was fondly referred to as the

"Needle of Kent" in honor of its tall, elegant spire that could be seen for miles around on a clear day. Regardless of the weather or day of the week, my father and mother frequently arranged to meet friends for a drink at one of their two favorite pubs or watering holes on the heath, one to be found just a few steps on each side of the church, so here's to "The Princess of Wales" and the "Hare and Billet," both establishments of great class!

There was good reason to celebrate in 1951 when it seemed appropriate to acknowledge all that had been accomplished in the short time since the end of the war in 1945. There had been many great changes put into place since then, including the much-celebrated National Health Service, which was launched in 1947 only two years after the end of the war. There had been a general acceptance from both political parties of the idea that it was absolutely the right and decent thing to put in place for the citizens, but it was the Labor government under the Prime Minister Mr. Clement Attlee who determinedly and finally pushed it through parliament to the great relief and appreciation of the English people. Even though there were still many deep scars, painful reminders, and difficult hardships for the people, rebuilding had begun. It was slow, but after six years the city was showing signs of recovery. Many new and important changes had been made, bombed cities were being rebuilt with a new architectural flair, infrastructure was repaired everywhere, and there was a general sense of relief and optimism in the air. The country needed to celebrate its new accomplishments, and so, with great fanfare, it was announced that there would be a Festival of Britain, one hundred years since the celebrations in 1851 of the Great Exhibition, which also celebrated the accomplishments of the arts, culture, and science, and at the young age of eleven years, I would play a small part in those celebrations.

It was decided that a new and architecturally exciting concert hall would make the main statement. Strategically placed on the southern embankment of the river Thames, this bold, new, modern building with its sensuous white curves soared, and with a combination of glass and wood, and an open interior plan, it also brought brightness, light, and thrilling acoustics and was a shining emblem of this festival that represented the beginning of a brave new period of restoration for England. It was named not surprisingly, the Royal Festival Hall. Not to be upstaged and an integral part of the 1951 celebrations was another great and handsome concert hall that stood in the west of London and would also participate in the general festival celebrations. A cherished Victorian landmark, it was known and loved affectionately by all Londoners as the home of the summer promenade concerts, an immensely

THE RELUCTANT IMMIGRANT

popular two month long series of orchestral concerts featuring the great musical repertoire, the stage being shared by different soloists and each of the five professional London orchestras. The Royal Albert Hall was to be the venue for another Festival of Britain event, a concert by the London Children's Chorus. It was decided that a few children from every elementary school in London would be the selected representatives of the city and become part of a London School's Choir formed to perform together in a special celebratory festival concert in the Royal Albert Hall. I was one of the couple of children selected from my school for this unforgettable experience, thanks to my wonderful teacher and coach, Anita Smith, who had singled me out for my singing voice when I was eight and had pushed me to perform on many occasions. Thirty-four years later, I would return to sing in the Royal Albert Hall, and once again Anita Smith would be in the audience.

There was an affordable abundance of activity and artistic choice in London at that time. The five famous and functioning orchestras performed at an array of fine concert halls around the city, and irresistible chamber music could also be found in exquisite, smaller venues many of which were lovely ancient churches oozing with architectural atmosphere where the music and the architecture blended together sympathetically. I heard great choruses sing music by great composers conducted by legendary conductors. The musical fireworks produced by the fabulous trio of the Israeli born, Daniel Barenboim, the recent Russian immigrant, Vladimir Ashkenazy and our very own young English prodigy Jacquline du Pre were among my favorites. I had seen Margo Fonteyn and Rudolf Nureyev, another gift from the Soviet era, leap together across the stage at Covent Garden, and I heard the greatest actors of the day perform everything from Shakespeare to Harold Pinter. I had swooned to the sound of a Beatle song and I couldn't live without the daily comfort and stimulation of the BBC! It seemed preposterous to me that I would have to leave all of that behind, and not at all what I had envisioned when three years earlier I had married Richard with his good looks, smarts, and a potential PhD under his arm. I was sure there were good jobs in England just waiting for him. So it was with a sinking, sickening feeling of unease and disquiet that I listened to him read the letter from a large corporation in America offering him a job in the city of Philadelphia. When he spread the large map of the United States onto our living room floor and pointed to where it was, sandwiched between New York and Washington, I felt sure it must be a sleepy, forgotten backwater in spite of its name and famed history.

I was not even curious; I felt as if I had left my soul behind. I was bewildered and confused, but I was here in the United States now and we were speeding southwest in this coach-size limo, with intersections and place names unknown to me, and strange traffic signs and signals I didn't recognize all flashing past, crisscrossing with major and minor road systems I didn't care about, and then finally, after five dizzying hours, we arrived at our destination, the small county town of Media, in the state of Pennsylvania. Although this town is old by American standards, nothing stood out that was special about the place except the amazing display of ugly, loopy, overhead hanging power cables visible at every intersection and along every street, looking like untidy black spaghetti that had been dropped in cart loads from above and had been left were they fell, forever ignored and apparently never noticed and never picked or tidied up. This was my first impression. In England all the power cables had been buried underground during various rebuilding phases as part of wise town planning to avoid the look of urban blight. Sadly I would have to get used to the "hanging black spaghetti" look because it was a feature visible everywhere, in small towns and large cities, across the whole country.

Realizing that my knowledge of Pennsylvania was sparse, I

made an effort to know more and discovered that the Quaker William Penn founded Media back in the sixteen hundreds, and although small, it must have once been a town of some importance because it became the county seat of Delaware County. It was located twelve miles west from the city of Philadelphia, which was a much larger city and one of considerable importance especially in the early history of the United States. It was also founded by the Englishman William Penn who came from an old Quaker family with early ties to King Charles II. The family had lived on an estate in England located in the county of Buckinghamshire, west of London, before they left for "the colonies" to escape the religious turmoil and intolerance that was rife in England at that time.

Our first resting place was the Media Inn, which did not merit its somewhat pretentious air, but it was to be home for a few weeks while we tried to settle in and find somewhere better to live, so we unpacked and began to explore our immediate surroundings, making an effort to enjoy and learn what we could and should learn about the place. One evening I was attempting to feed the children in the stuffy, fake-wood paneled restaurant of the Media Inn, before the businessmen arrived for food and drink, and was having difficulty controlling one-year-old Andrew who had recently discovered the tactile pleasure of grabbing a handful of whatever soft food was on his plate and throwing it as far as he could in any direction. As luck would have it, Richard had arrived back early from his first day at General Electric and at this very crucial moment was standing at the restaurant entrance watching the scene. "Help me," I mouthed with mounting desperation since Beth had now emptied a glass of milk all over the tablecloth. "I can't," he said. "They won't let me in without a jacket!"

Media was the county seat of Delaware County. It had a couple of municipal buildings, a small courthouse, a small library, a few car dealerships, and fast-food joints, but it was disappointingly scruffy. The sidewalks were mostly cracked, and weeds grew abundantly through the cracks and nobody seemed to walk anywhere, perhaps because it wasn't very pleasurable, and everyone drove for even the shortest of distances anyway. All I could see were the heads of people sitting in the driving seat of very large cars. In those early days in America, I had the feeling that my life resembled a chapter out of Alice, in not-so-wonderful Wonderland. I recognized things around me, could give them a name, but when I looked closer or listened harder, I realized it wasn't always the correct name and so I often didn't understand what was being said to me or even where I was.

Why was the language so deceptively different and shopping for our first essential purchases so challenging? I thought Americans spoke English, but I was wrong. Actual words and certainly pronunciation were different, some differences were logical, others confusing for example a pushchair I found out in American is a stroller, a pavement is a sidewalk, petrol is gas, etc. A visit to the grocery shop, "store," was perplexing. A popular detergent in England was called Daz, but in America it was Duz. Multiply this a hundred times and I began to feel both mentally challenged and emotionally confused. Which I was! It took months of determination to conquer or at least feel moderately accomplished in this new language so that I could shop and feed my family, confident I wasn't poisoning them.

In the sweaty, heady heat of early June, I pushed the children in their pushchair or stroller along the cracking pavement or sidewalk in search of other human beings. But it appeared there were none. Not a soul. There was nobody to say "good morning" or "hi" or "hello" to. People simply didn't walk anywhere here in deep suburbia. Streams of cars followed each other on the *wrong* side of the road with a human head bobbing and looking blankly and obliviously straight ahead. There didn't appear to be a designated safety crossing sign anywhere so you had to take your life and the lives of your children into your own hands and worm your way cautiously across this dangerous onslaught of vehicles whose drivers had no intention of stopping for you. As a pedestrian you were forced to trespass into the domain of the ever-moving motor car, and if you got in the way, they seemed to think they were perfectly within their right to run right over you, or at least sound (honk) their horn. Oh, I so missed the friendly crossing guard or policeman standing beside the flashing Belisha beacon and the black-and-white Zebra striped, painted path holding his big red STOP sign high for all to see, stopping the traffic in all directions while guiding pedestrians safely across to the other side of the road.

The intense oppressive heat continued in earnest as I went for my solitary stroll with the children to a local park that had few attractions, and I soon realized that we had better return to the chilly but now welcome air conditioning of the Media Inn because it was already much too hot, humid, and unhealthy to be out of doors. We were not used to such a sweltering climate. At home seventy degrees Fahrenheit was considered "very hot" but here we were dealing with eighty-five to ninety degrees Fahrenheit with a saturating, draining humidity, and this was still only the month of June!

One month before we left England for the United States, on April 4, 1968, the great religious civil rights leader Martin Luther King was cruelly slain with an assassin's bullet in Memphis, Tennessee. I think that this ever-present display of senseless violence was one of the main reasons I felt so uneasy about moving to the United States. I thought of it as a violent country that still lived by "Wild West" rules. Now again, just a few weeks after we had arrived in the US, it happened to another great man who had devoted himself to working tirelessly to help those less fortunate than himself and who promised to be a shining light on the political platform. On June 5, 1968, Robert F. Kennedy was brutally gunned down in California having just won the Californian primary election for the Democratic nomination for president of the United States. Just six years earlier in 1962, I remember sitting in my living room in our London house listening to the evening news and weeping on hearing the horrible news from America that his brother President John Kennedy had been murdered. I think it would be true to say the whole world was overwhelmed with grief and struck hard with horror and disbelief over the sickening, shooting murder of President John Fitzgerald Kennedy, Robert Kennedy's own brother. Both men offered great skill, hope, and promise not only to their own citizens but to their influence on the world community. Their loss was immeasurable.

There was no need for gun ownership in Britain. Gun ownership was relatively unheard of except for wealthy citizens who lived in the country in large luxurious but drafty houses that had been in their family for many generations. Often the land was more valuable and luscious than the house that occupied it. "Shooting parties" had been traditional for centuries where groups of hunters would track deer or other smaller wild edible animals for the simple purpose of killing them with a bullet, while keeping the animal population under control, but numbers seemed to be a secondary consideration. Most of the British populace thought the whole thing cruel and barbaric, and many would often gather in large organized groups to demonstrate and generally annoy the shooters. They were animal lovers and were anti-vivisection supporters.

I mention this to demonstrate the real horror and puzzlement felt by the vast majority of the British people when looking at America's apparent love affair and easy access to fire arms—the ever-constant threat of the gun! This constant threat and effect of the gun is brutally demonstrated on a daily basis, over and over again, shattering lives of families and communities across the country, forever. This ever-present display of senseless violence made me feel a sadness and despair and question what civility really meant, and indeed, the question could be asked, how can a nation that relies so heavily on weaponry, and vigilante expression, call itself truly civilized? What applied historically in a written document under different circumstances does not have to be dragged into a modern society and considered sacrosanct—surely rules and laws needed to be adjusted as societies changed and developed, and what might have made sense two hundred years ago when a "Wild West" mentality prevailed did not necessarily make common sense in modern times.

As I write this remembrance forty years on when violence has deteriorated to even more deplorable levels it's obvious we really do have an armed citizenry now and I shake my head in disbelief at the stupidity of the laws and the keepers and makers of those laws that allow this behavior to demean this great country so deeply. Citizens who feel they need to always carry a gun, like an emotional crutch, must be very insecure and unsure of themselves as individuals. I can't see that it has much to do with the country's history and the fact that gun advocates claim it was written in a document two hundred years ago doesn't mean that it continues to be a relevant necessity today. Historical documents tell us of events and decisions made at different periods in time, where different priorities and behavior applied. That surely does not automatically mean that the same behavior is appropriate or desirable in a modern society. After all, spitting in public was generally accepted in those far off days, but we have learnt that it is unacceptable today mostly because it is a disease carrier. Guns carry death too.

Moving on, we gave notice at the Media Inn after one month. They were very polite but I think they were pleased to see us leave and muttered something about needing to redecorate the dining room. Good news arrived about new accommodation. An apartment had been found in a neighboring area called Prospect

Park. I will not dwell long on this new and unusual experience. I mention it only in passing. Prospect Park made Media look like a shining city on a hill, gentrified and up-market in every way, which I later realized it probably was and had been all along, but in those stark early days of general bewilderment, I was hostile to everything. I found that my new neighbors in Prospect Park were hardworking people, and they never shirked that hard work, meaning that life was not in any way easy for them, but they welcomed us warmly, for which I still thank them.

Despondent in the small dingy apartment, I felt dumped there for the purpose of giving entertainment to the local residents. Everyone stared at us unabashedly for a few days, huddling in clusters, muttering inaudibly, but never threateningly. Apart from day-to-day courtesies, we had little in common, except the closeness that comes in a small community when all the children, including mine, share the same head lice along with a nasty little pest that burrows deep under the skin and sucks your child's blood! But an inquisitive and uncomplaining neighbor who had few teeth but an ever-cheerful and undaunted smile, was known to everyone as Peg Leg Patty, and she had been elected as the spokeswoman of the group, and she was an angel. She had lost a leg above the knee in an accident, which she didn't want to talk about. She had to strap on a pink artificial leg, which she sometimes wore, but mostly didn't because it was a bad fit and she was more comfortable without it, on crutches. Peg Leg Patty, a term of endearment given to her by her neighbors, had a font of experience in all things crawly, challenging, and nasty in life and came to my rescue with remedies for the nasty things in the children's hair and under their skin and consoled them with sweet biscuits and, for me, dark, warm, very sweet coffee almost daily. I will never forget her!

CHAPTER ONE
PART TWO

Robin Hill

Robin Hill! Through a great stroke of luck and being in the right place at the right time, we were able to rent a wonderful rustic house that stood on an acre of grassy land at the top of a graceful and secluded spot just outside Media, called Robin Hill. Here I was able to take a deep breath, smile again, and begin to heal a little. The house was owned by two University of Pennsylvania professors who were leaving on sabbatical for a year. An Englishman, a neighbor, who worked for the company with Richard heard about our housing plight and approached the owners about the possibility of renting to us. The two dear doctors were delighted to help, and in a short space of time, we moved in. The house was an unfussy, rather rustic, wooden, A-frame structure. The interior was modestly and comfortably furnished and looked as though many children had been fortunate enough to have it as their home for many years. I was told to relax and not worry about my children hurting the place because it was indestructible.

The house stood high up on the top of Robin Hill, and access to the top of the hill was a narrow, one-car-wide lane, barely visible from the road below, which curved its way gently and gracefully to the top, which was where our new home stood. There was a beautiful view from every window and an enormous soft green grassy lawn that cascaded back down the hill. I was tearfully grateful and flitted around unpacking, poking into cupboards, allocating bedrooms, and peaking at the many books in the cozy, comfortable library.

After a day or two, a handsome young boy from a neighbor's house knocked at the door to greet us with the valuable information that he was the local mouse-catcher and that we probably had a few of the little darlings in our basement, but not to worry he only lived next door and was on call practically round the clock, and he charged ten cents a tail. He immediately got to work in our basement where, he told me, he had been many times before, and I immediately paid him ten cents. He had a bounce to his walk and he resolutely bounced back into his house obviously pleased to have new business opportunities just one house down the hill.

Later that day I discovered I had delightfully welcoming neighbors who arrived at my door to introduce themselves with warm, out-of-the-oven cookies, or biscuits, and a pitcher of "iced (strange) tea." A small girl with large eyes and dark hair and her mouse-catcher brother stood beside their smiling parents, who greeted us in a soft, southern drawl that I couldn't at first understand. They were the Powells, Luther, Lou, Marty, and Donna from Louisiana, and they lived in the house next door and were kindness itself.

I was relieved to be somewhat settled at least for a while, the lease was for a year. But I was still unsettled in myself and had difficulty falling asleep and then slept fitfully, waking up wondering where I was and what I was doing there. All the changes and moves were impacting the children and they were not sleeping well and were fussing with their food and things generally.

Thinking myself to be a caring and responsible parent I was horrified when my back was turned, to find that my adventurous, sixteen-month-old toddling son Anthony had managed to climb to the top of a flight of wooden stairs and then had inevitably fallen back down putting his two new precious front teeth through his bottom lip, which gushed volumes of blood, requiring a panicky rush to the local hospital for three stitches. Continuing his exploring adventures undeterred, he gave me daily scares and I needed eyes in the back of my head at all times. We were playing a sneaky game, and when I blinked, he quietly managed to find a way to climb up onto the top of the upright piano, where I found him full of pride and grinning with glee. He did grow up to be an accomplished and entertaining pianist so he must have had an inquisitive flair for the piano early on.

Beth was a demure, adorable, blue-eyed little girl who was nearly four years old. She was an enthusiastic early reader and it was always easy to occupy her with interesting activities. She was a few years younger than our neighbor's daughter Donna, and I think Beth enjoyed having the attention of an older "sister" next door, and they played well and nicely together, which made her happy and so I was happy too. Nelva-Lou was a happy and always cheerful woman a few years younger than me, who gave me lots of useful information about the area, day care, and where I could find different daily items from various shops or stores, and "supermarkets"—where the long aisles with items for sale went on for miles. But I found everything was spread out in a sprawl, the "High Street" shopping as I knew it didn't exist and a car was essential to get to all the different places.

The Powells cooked a wonderful welcome barbecue for us one weekend and introduced us to some "real" southern cooking with rich, tasty sauces, unusual flavors and delicacies from the South, all of it was delicious and different. At one point the word "grits" came into my vocabulary, being offered as the starch portion in a savory dish, but in consistency it reminded me of semolina. Grits are made from a coarsely ground corn and has salt added whereas semolina is made from a purified wheat base, and in England, it is eaten with milk and honey for breakfast. Many things were similar, but not the same.

Lou and Luther were very hospitable and keen to show us some of the local beauty spots. I fell in love with two of them, and feeling a passion rush back into my body and my life again gave me a surge of hope. A short drive from Robin Hill is the Tyler Arboretum. This breathtaking beauty spot is one of the oldest arboreta in the northeast and consists of 650 acres of champion trees set beside acres of flowering shrubs, a diverse horticulture, renowned for its rare plant collections, small streams, and an undulating landscape that rolls endlessly into the distance. Once we had discovered this wild and natural togetherness, this quiet un-peopled gem, we explored it every week and saw with amazement and joy the slow seasonal changes as they unfolded. It even came with a long pedigree history. Again, William Penn, our Englishman from Buckinghamshire, had been here before us! He signed a "lease and release" agreement for property in Pennsylvania that contained the site now occupied by the Arboretum. Families involved with the arboretum date back to the 1600s. Things were becoming more interesting for me.

"With watercolor, you can pick up the atmosphere, the temperature, the sound of snow shifting through the trees or over the ice of a small pond or against a windowpane. Watercolor perfectly expresses the free side of my nature," so said the great painter Andrew Wyeth who still lived and worked less than twenty miles from Media, but, of whom, regrettably, I had never heard. Discovering his work permanently exhibited at the Brandywine Museum in Chadds Ford, where he and his family had lived for generations, took my breath away; it was so profound.

He was able to achieve a poignancy and restraint that almost quivered before my eyes. His technique was original. I had never, in all my gallery wonderings, seen such work. It was, on the one hand, minimalist, but it also contained a warmth and an intensity that drew you into the subject while at the same time made you want to avert your eyes—it was so personal. Landscapes were stripped down to the barest necessity and the solitary figures leaned into the background silently, almost unnoticed, with an increased importance of emotion, "transmitting a sense of loneliness." At this time in my life, I think on a deep level I identified with them.

My parents were pining for me and their grandchildren and so it was with great joy to read a letter announcing their plans for a visit early in September, just a few months away. My father, a sports journalist, was accompanying an English rugby team who would play in a tournament that would include teams in Philadelphia and Washington. I was thrilled and so excited at the prospect of seeing them but knew it would be an emotional visit. However, now I was in a position to be positive about where we were living and had some local knowledge that I was proud about, and I looked forward to sharing my new environment with them.

I had a long list of desired items I was desperately missing but couldn't find anywhere in my local shops, like tea. Not a beverage of choice in the United States in the sixties, and so the miserable selection available was without any resemblance to English tea which by comparison was rich and dark and full of flavor, and I had been having withdrawal symptoms for months. My mum, as opposed to "mom" would also bring favorite biscuits or cookies, After Eight Mint chocolates, marmite, an English essential but impossible to describe accurately. It was a thick, sticky, black, salty, savory, smelly substance with yeast being its main ingredient, being a good flavorful addition to meaty casseroles but also tasty when spread thinly on toast or crackers. Caution to readers, I never met a single American who, if they ever bought it, it was only once and it was thought to be absolutely revolting! A strange, very English acquired taste! I also begged for clothing items from Marks and Spencer's for the children and for me, the chain store that sold attractive, affordable, high-quality, conventional clothing, which the whole nation seemed to wear happily, so everyone looked like a version of someone they knew who just happened to belong to the same club, which, of course they did. It was copycat shopping, which everyone approved of, and they liked it that way, happily admiring each other's purchases, declaring that they had one "just like that too!" I couldn't wait for my "care package." This one-way parcel system of essential "care giving" to an English family pining for items from home and regularly in need, but three thousand miles away in the great US of A, went on every few months from the London shops to wherever I happened to be living for the next twenty years. By which time the United States had at last caught up with a serious flair for fashion which happily ended the fuddy-duddy era and delicacies like Typhoo Tea and After Eight Chocolate Mints and even Marmite could be found fairly easily on American shelves. Progress! Oh, such relief and joy!

I was beside myself with excitement as we drove to JFK airport in New York in our new, enormous white station wagon to meet my parents. Tears and happiness abounded on both sides as they came through the barrier.

It was wonderful to be reunited. My parents glowed with joy at seeing us all. We hugged and kissed and wiped away pent-up tears, talking and catching up, our words bubbling and spilling uncontrollably from our lips. I wanted so much to reassure them and have them remember us as being happy in this new country, even though the feeling of homesickness, like a dull headache, felt ever present.

We took them everywhere. They were both thrilled and enthusiastic about everything they saw and commented, as most

Europeans do, about the large size of everything and the "wide open spaces" everywhere. I wanted my parents to feel that I was more than just coping in my new surroundings, even though in my heart I didn't feel it. I wanted them to believe that life was good for me so I set out to show them things that would impress them. They commented on the eye-popping food portions in restaurants, neck-breaking skyscraper buildings in New York, enormous automobiles, cheap petrol or gasoline, wide roads and highways with multiple lanes, inexpensive food prices, freezing cold air conditioning everywhere. They walked up Fifth Avenue, jaws dropping with admiration, "tickled pink" they were by everything. Dad was photographed leaning against Jack Dempsey's bar. Mum loved the grace of Central Park (but she touched my arm and quietly reminded me, that "you know, dear, we have five parks this size in the center of London!" Touché! They described Philadelphia as "shabbily graceful" and were surprised that the city had such an extensive area of handsome eighteenth-century buildings and thought that the beauty and simplicity of Independence Hall and the quiet but powerful story it told was the best. Washington was next on the grand tour and they were emotionally stilled by this capital city with its quiet grandeur and the surprising French architectural influence, courtesy of Pierre L'Enfant, with all the buildings offering a more "human scale" to those they had seen in the New York skyscrapers. They enjoyed the many monuments and museums the city offered and agreed they were all very impressive. But they found it was difficult to keep adjusting to the outside extreme heat and humidity and the ice-cold chill of air conditioning on the inside, and by now the constant changing of temperature was getting to them and they frequently needed to sit and sip something refreshing.

The days were slipping by quickly and without mentioning it we were all aware that our time together was running out as their return date loomed large on the calendar. I had left my local sight-seeing finds until last, the Tyler Arboretum, Longwood Gardens, and Andrew Wyeth museum were only half-day excursions, so we had more time to sit together and watch the children play and thrill on the big swing that hung low from an enormous old oak tree on the lawn at Robin Hill, reminding us of the beautiful paining called The Swing by the eighteenth-century French artist Jean-Honere Fragonard displayed at the Wallace Collection in London.

Departure day inevitably arrived but the children were young and didn't understand the full impact on our emotions, so we tried to stay cheerful for their sake and their childish chatter helped to cheer us on the journey back to New York. Once at the airport, you don't have much time to weep, as you are inevitably swept along by the efficiency of the process (this is 1968), which delivers you finally to the departure gate. None of us wanted a prolonged wailing event to be our last memory of the visit, so with typical British stiff-upper-lip style, a quick, loving kiss and hug, and a "see you soon," they disappeared through the barrier.

◈

The following days were quiet ones for me as I enjoyed going over my parents' visit in all its detail, lingering over the numerous photographs I would make copies of, feeling generally pleased, and declaring the whole visit a tremendous success. Now there was a different kind of space to deal with once again, and three thousand miles was a lot of space.

At the suggestion of the English wife of Richard's colleague I had arranged for Beth to start a nursery school close by. Grace was a kind, busy, rather bustling but happy and practical lady who lived close by and offered her teenage daughter as a baby sitter should we need one. After about eight years in the United States, Grace had lost her English accent and had obviously embraced the more material lifestyle wholeheartedly. I was encouraged and perplexed at the same time.

We were also invited to dinner parties in the area by colleagues who worked with Richard. They were very hospitable people living in large, by English standards, houses with grassy, manicured lawns and sometimes even a swimming pool. I wore my new London best dresses, which had hemlines four to five inches above the knee, thinking nothing of it; it was a "mini skirt" after all and all the rage in London. I had just come from what was still being referred to as "Swinging London," which was a wild and colorful city where everyone expressed themselves in wild and colorful clothes. The men obviously liked what I was wearing, but the rather mature matrons of Media, a kind but fuddy-duddy group of wives, with their hair tightly and permanently curled, were a little taken aback. The conversations inevitably divided between the men talking shop and the women talking recipes and shopping. I don't mean exciting shopping. I mean food shopping! I couldn't see myself as a member of this group and realized we had better do some exploring of alternative places to live when the lease on Robin Hill, now galloping forward fast, was up. When I mentioned politely that we might look across the river in New Jersey for a house, you could hear a pin drop, followed by a loud "group inhalation" sound of disapproval. "You can't live in New Jersey," seemed to be the unanimous cry. We'll see, I thought.

We were now deeply immersed in a new and beautiful season of the year which had arrived as autumn or fall, but it took me quite off guard. Being used as I was to "the season of mists and mellow fruitfulness" of Wordsworth's poem, this autumn was quite different. The heat-draining days of sweat and airless air had happily melted away to be replaced in the early morning by mists, thin and tantalizing in their delicacy. By mid to late morning they had evaporated to be replaced by brilliant sunshine, bold and hot, set against a cloudless deep blue sky. The colors were different too. Nothing mellow here. These colors were brazen in their audacity. Shocking colors shouted out, in bright scarlet, orange, and ten shades of yellow. They blazed across the landscape defying the encroaching darkness of winter. Clearly this was a favorite season with everyone. The weather was energizing, and you could feel it in your body as it pushed you to move faster, squeeze more jobs and activities into the day, sleep more peacefully at night. I loved it.

As we walked in our favorite place, we attempted to give the first biology lessons in entropy to Beth and Andrew as we pointed out to them the fallen trees and falling leaves in the Tyler arboretum and how they had changed from being trees and were now going back into the earth to nourish other growing things that we would see and enjoy next spring.

We also began to explore the city of Philadelphia and enjoyed the concerts played by the Philadelphia Orchestra conducted by Eugene Ormandy. Renowned for its lush string section, which gave it a gorgeous, easily recognized Philadelphia sound, the great orchestra did not disappoint. They were world class. We had brought with us LP recordings by this orchestra being conducted by Maestro Eugene Ormandy so it was a thrill to hear them live in their beautiful old concert hall, the Academy of Music with its comfortable red plush seating, gilt trim, and rich chandeliers. This majestic concert hall was built by Napoleon LeBrun in 1857, modeling the lavish interior on the La Scala Opera House in Milan. The Academy of Music is the oldest known concert and opera house in continuous use in the United States and great conductors of the nineteenth century introduced many memorable first performances in this impressive space. It was a thrill and a privilege to be there.

We tried to find some interesting restaurants, but back in the late sixties, Philadelphia suffered from being too close to buzzy

New York, which had all the action in terms of many of the arts and great restaurants. But Philadelphia was "old" by American standards, and we enjoyed wandering east of Broad Street toward the Delaware River, discovering delightful narrow and cobbled streets like Pine and Spruce, displaying architectural gems of eighteenth century with houses and churches still in good use. Farther uptown, and later in period was "the old lady of Broad Street," the Academy of Music, and a few blocks farther on was wealthy property facing what could have been a beautiful area to sit and muse, but this prime piece of land looked poor and sadly neglected, lacking essential flowering borders or anything of inspiring horticulture. I thought what a disappointment Rittenhouse Square was. Every neighborhood in London has a public square tended lovingly by locals and city alike with borders abundant with seasonal flowers and shrubs for the public to enjoy. Perhaps I had missed its renaissance, but in 1968, Rittenhouse Square made me frown, where were the public beautifiers or even a few local private ones? Has this scruffy public space ever had the attention it deserved and enjoyed a real renaissance? It could be a place to be envied but it continues to be disappointing in its plantings and borders and remains a wasted opportunity to make the largest square in the city a real beauty. Londoners would be crawling all over this space, planting and beautifying, so important in a large, noisy, and polluted city. A saving grace that was close by was the lovely building that was the home of the Curtis Institute of Music set on one corner of the square on Locust Street, and with its windows open wide to the autumn air, a passerby could hear the exquisite soft sounds of soprano voices trilling and pianos tickling as students, preparing one day to be famous names, were being put through their vocal and instrumental paces by others, whose names were already famous.

The Philadelphia Museum of Art held an awesome position in the city, standing high like an ancient Greek temple at the end of an attractive green boulevard or parkway where the flags from all the nations fluttered in display on either side. The artworks on display inside the museum were all notable, and every period was generously represented. I enjoyed this museum and we visited often.

We were disappointed to discover that hardly anyone we now knew from the Media suburbs hardly ever ventured into the city at all. Philadelphia was called the "City of Brotherly Love." My friend William Penn named it and called it his "greene countrie towne." The motto has been adapted slightly from the Greek meaning "brotherly love"—*philos* meaning "love or friendship" and *adelphos* meaning "brother." It is a fine name and perhaps the early Quakers upheld this meaning in a worthy way. However, that didn't sufficiently encourage any of the suburbanites we had met to venture forth very often to enjoy the pleasures of the city, rather the city was to be generally avoided. Perhaps I was wrong but I suspected that the real reason for their suspicions was the high population of poor African Americans living there, and in their mind that fact caused the city to be a decidedly undesirable place.

Our first Christmas crept upon us and I dithered around trying to reconstruct what I knew and loved about a traditional English Christmas. Obviously an English Christmas has a much longer history to it with regard to the religious celebrations associated with the season than America does, and although church attendance is very low in England compared with America, the English have over the centuries pulled together a unifying and rich variety of traditional delights from food and music, dance, decoration, games, and general merriment, all of which you will find shared each Christmas season, in the same way in every home, large or small, across the land.

In my preparations leading up to Christmas—or the holidays, as they are called in America because it also includes the

Jewish holiday of Hanukkah and other religious celebrations, it was not so easy for me to find a turkey for our English Christmas feast. This was because most Americans prefer ham and even beef, and traditionally turkeys are eaten a few weeks earlier for the Thanksgiving dinner in remembrance of the first pilgrims in Massachusetts, where they were in plentiful supply, and who ate them to commemorate their first year in America. But Christmas was our turn and although three thousand miles from home, we ate turkey with everyone else in England. Among other "sweet meats" for an English Christmas desert, the traditional "Christmas" pudding is everyone's favorite. It used to be called a plum pudding, a similar recipe made famous by Charles Dickens, in *A Christmas Carol*. It is made from a mixture of suet, eggs, flour, and mixed dried fruit and with a generous measure of whiskey, and where a lucky person could even find a silver sixpence while chewing, or alternatively, unlucky, if a tooth finds the sixpence and is broken in the process! Once, when I was young, just one time, I made one of these monster deserts from scratch, following a traditional recipe, which was ten pages long and demanded ridiculous items like a half a spoon of grated carrot, which I couldn't imagine making the slightest difference to any part of the puddings' taste or appearance, and I can tell you, it didn't! Wrapped in cloth and steamed, it emerged looking like a cannon ball, a round dark, sticky pudding wreaking of the whiskey, from the mixture itself, and then when cooked, it received a final dousing all over its outside. Finally a match is struck, which turns it into a flaming ball of yummy delight as it goes off on its triumphant paraded with great fanfare and a chorus of cheers from the eager guests, while dangerously blazing and burning the symbolic "sprig of holly" stuck into its center for decoration, on its journey to the table. Yes, it might sound a little unappetizing for the faint of heart or stomach, but it is an essential item for the traditional English Christmas and certainly one tradition really worth preserving.

Another essential, frivolous but very silly decorative item for the dinner table are Christmas "crackers." This, happily, is not an edible item. It is made from decorative paper, which is rolled up, allowing space inside for a silly paper hat that must be worn, no excuses. Also included is a boring puzzle game, but the best fun and cause of the hilarious laughter and general childish behavior from everyone, young and especially old, occurs when two people pull at each end of the cracker, causing a loud cracking sound as the paper rips apart and the strip hidden inside "explodes." In many respects the English celebrated a day based more on ancient revelry and the great influence of Charles Dickens and even earlier influences, including strange medieval traditions, than anything that was very religious, that is except for the music. American Christmas seemed overly commercialized by comparison with the shopping frenzy starting months earlier than in England with too many renditions of *White Christmas* and other sentimental seasonal songs as the constant musical backdrop.

However, even without all of those reconstructed essential English traditions available, that first Christmas in America and especially in Robin Hill was beautiful, and we had a guest. A stray, single young man, fresh off the boat from UK who, among so many, had also been plucked from the brightest and the best minds in England, along with Richard, which was why the period back then was called "the brain drain." But he was homesick as well and we all ate and drank and reminisced about Christmas back home.

We missed the warm, welcoming pubs with cheap "fairy" lights around the bar. Inevitably a sprig of mistletoe hanging from an unavoidable door lintel and fresh holly galore distributed in generous clumps anywhere and everywhere.

Many nonbelievers would also flock to the ancient churches and the cathedrals for the atmosphere and out of reverence for the generations that had trodden their weary way before them and worn away the great slabs of flagstone flooring, but also because of the human warmth that pervades in these otherwise chilly mansions built to heaven. One can feel the humanity spread across the length and breadth of the old land, glorious and ancient traditional music is played and sung by stunningly beautiful boy soprano voices, very many of these broadcast live and then recorded for later listening pleasure on BBC radio. The huge Norwegian fir tree, a traditional gift from Norway, stood in the middle of Trafalgar Square smothered in colorful lights and groups of impromptu singers would serenade the shoppers, who weighed down with packages, were struggling cheerfully for busses and trains, homeward bound. It was more fun to bustle along in the crowded streets of shoppers and revelers, and the walkers pitied those who resorted to driving a car, which immediately cut them off from all human fun and collective seasonal cheer.

Regent Street was the most extravagant display of street lighting, which lit up the late afternoon dusk and kept going all night. Christmas Eve was the best. All shopping done, everyone seemed to be rushing home, making sure not to miss one of the great musical events of the year.

At 4:00 p.m. on Christmas Eve, the great choir of Kings College Chapel, in Cambridge began The Nine Lessons and Carols. Many people queued and waited from the night before to be sure of a place in what was the official high point of the celebrations leading up to Christmas. The chapel was started by King Henry VI in 1446 and took over a century to build. It has the largest and most beautiful fan vault ceiling in the world and some of the finest medieval stained glass windows. Probably, also, the most famous cathedral choir in the world, and this event trumped all others in the beauty of the music with carols mostly old but always with a few new introductions, and in the readings from the Bible. Local people in soft regional accents alternated readings with members of the church. The service is an ancient tradition in a country where since the early fifties church attendance has fluctuated, in London mostly downward, falling to 30 percent of the population who were regular church goers. What replaced official church doctrine in many places was a quiet, internal calm, a personal, common sense spirituality, based not on religion, but on a respect for the improvement of the human condition. For the two thousand years of history going back to the Romans, populations have persevered against great odds, the frequent savagery of war, recovery, and the continuous spirit of never giving up, our ancestors had been dragging themselves generation after generation through the mire, on the long journey forward producing the fine, enduring qualities of mankind–great architecture, literature, music, philosophy, science–indeed all knowledge that came from that endurance, the determination and the endeavor of the human spirit, fighting against ignorance and oppression, one painful step after another, two steps forward and frequently another one backward but all the time some progress was made for humanity and the great surge forward continued unabated through the centuries. That is the human spirituality and belief I saw in the eyes of my countrymen and women and that is what brought us together to celebrate the tradition on Christmas Eve. There was another, I believe, for the on-going turning away from a belief in a "God" philosophy. It was because something snapped in the minds of many in the population during the First World War and a great rage came upon the people. Rage against the German Kaiser, rage against the English established church and religious leaders, rage against the British upper class establishment, all responsible for driving forward and forcing what became the hideous slaughter and carnage of the First World War, lasting for four years and followed twenty years later by a repeat performance with the Second World War when once again the allied forces were forced this time to "finish the job" with Hitler and the German fascists. From the blood, desolate hope, death, disgust, and utter dissolution of these horrible wars many of the people simply turned away from the idea of a loving god, or any form of a higher being. The upper class and the church on both sides of the battle always believed that "God was on their side, and they wore the words on their uniform and uttered them in their prayers. But for the men in the trenches and on the battlefield in the middle of the mud and carnage, it must have seemed to them that God was nowhere to be seen. They turned a new page with an old philosophy and instead embraced the truly sustainable and consoling emotions based on the endurance of common humanity. Quoting part of the courageous words of the first World War, a poet who was himself killed in action, Seigfried Sassoon made a defiant statement in 1917, called 'A Soldier's Declaration': 'I am making this statement as an act of willful defiance of military authority, because I believe the war is being deliberately prolonged by those who have the power to end it!'"

Back with gentler thoughts and the softly falling snow in Robin Hill, the children already in their dreamy slumbers, the three of us sat at the table in front of the large picture window. This was like a small American Christmas gift to us because although we sang hopefully for a "White Christmas," it rarely snowed in England. The children were asleep waiting for Father Christmas (Santa Claus) in their dreams and we sat in candle light and watched the large flakes of snow fall fast and heavily, lit by the light on the deck outside. Yes, it was beautiful as we watched and listened to deeply familiar Christmas music from among the great pile of LP's we had dragged across the wide ocean, just for a moment like this, music written hundreds of years ago, warming our spirits and making us homesick for those familiar things of Christmas back home. Snow as deep and crisp and even as in the Good King Wenceslas carol on the "Feast of Stephen." Heavy snow like this almost never fell in England, although many wished it would to give the season that extra special magic touch.

Sometimes at home, our hopes were raised then dashed because the snow predicted would only be a dusting and disappeared in an hour. It was a novelty for us to have this much snow, up to twelve inches deep, but in Media this amount was a usual winter event. For us this was a happening of grand proportions, and because it was also very cold, the snow stayed on the rooftops and pavements or sidewalks for weeks and outlined every twig, branch, and tree limb. The local authorities had a budget for snow removal so that roads could be cleared and the traffic could move unhampered while mountainous piles of frozen snow decorated every street corner.

※

Still snowing the following morning it became a child's paradise and Robin Hill was perfectly poised to be the local favorite winter sport center and kids grabbed anything they could sit on and that would slide with gathering speed down the hill. All houses had central heating so it was cozy and warm inside, and most houses also had fireplaces, when on occasions like this, arms full of logs were lugged up the hill to burn brightly in the fireplace; there was a romance to the whole event. England has a more temperate climate, and the soil doesn't freeze and so by early February signs of life begin to peak through the earth, but here in Pennsylvania spring came tantalizingly late, and by March people were aching for the signs of spring and everyone was praying that there would be no more heavy snow because local funding for removal had run out, and the snow had now turned to an ugly, dirty black slushy mess. But it was a big event for us, and it was good, even wonderful while it lasted. But lurking under the melting snow was a burning social problem that was unnerving.

While I pondered daily over the large and perplexing changes and adjustments that had happened to me personally and to my own family in the year of 1968, I was also keeping track throughout that year and in another part of my consciousness of the great turmoil and anger that was erupting in many areas of the world and could not be ignored. From the many contributions to lectures on twentieth century Europe entitled "The Year of the Barricades" an attempt is made to explain why in the sixties, with little warning, the youth of Europe and America were aflame with fury, which came to a head in 1968, which was known as the "year of revolution." It was, among other things, a moral revolt—"a revolt of passion in the interests of humanity." Following the decade after the end of WWII, there had been a steady recovery and conformity in the 1950s, and it was perplexing for everyone when this rage suddenly erupted, without the help of the social media, when tens of thousands of students in universities in New York, California, London, Prague, Poland, Berlin, Rome, and Paris exploded onto the streets and went on a continuous violent strike against the establishment both of their universities and their governments alike. The French government was temporarily paralyzed by the most severe social protest movement since the days of the Paris Commune in 1871 when the student strike took over the Sorbonne. Administration buildings at the London School of Economics in London were occupied by protesting students. And as all this took place Soviet tanks rolled into Prague, in an attempt to break up the students' street demonstrations, an event known as the Prague Spring. The appalling massacre at My Lai was only one of similar episodes that occurred in Vietnam and among the many protests a deeply personal event took place in Central Park in New York City, when a ninety-two-year-old woman, a Quaker, set herself on fire, making the ultimate sacrifice and protest of the war in Vietnam. To say it was an ugly, violent, and passionate period is an understatement! Sociologists have written reams in an attempt to explain this lengthy and unnerving phenomenon that had quickly spread like a virus, and mostly they agreed that the most important factor for the students of both Europe and America was the ongoing horror of the Vietnam War. To them it was worse than a blunder. It was a crime, and Kennedy and Johnson were to share near-total responsibility for the escalation of the war, but as it dragged on in 1968, the responsibility passed on and Richard Nixon who was also implicated.

Across the country young men burned their draft cards on the steps of their local Selective Service office. Crowds chanted, "Hell no, we won't go," or "hey, hey, LBJ, how many kids did you kill today?" The protesters saw that the governments of Europe were implicit in the blame as well–after all, Vietnam had been a French problem before it was inherited by the United States. As the students saw it, their collective protests were against many forms of tyranny including the big one—the old "cold war" mentality that viewed Southeast Asia as a breeding ground for international communism and nothing would be spared until it had been completely crushed. Added to this frightening era of domestic and foreign violence, we must remember the battleground that developed at the 1968 Democratic National Convention, which ended with the tragic murder of Bobby Kennedy, following just a few months after the assassination of Dr. Martin Luther King Jr. Although England was, of course, touched by the same escalating student protests seen everywhere, I still felt it was fundamentally a calmer, safer place for me and for my family to be living, and although I struggled, fairly, to come to terms with my new surroundings, I thought that the events everywhere were deeply disturbing, and it seemed even more unstable here in America, where I had just arrived.

The New Year found our worried minds looking with mixed feelings toward the end of our lease. Robin Hill had been a lovely place to live for a while and it gave me time to breathe and heal, and although still very homesick, I knew another move was necessary. Yes, the suburbs were lovely and I had made a few friends, but it also felt stuffy and conservative and all the homes were too expensive and I felt there was something vaguely oppressive there.

Discussions about the Vietnam War seemed to have been airbrushed away, and any reference to, or about the "the war" were uncomfortable and silenced and the subject quickly changed. Against all advice, but feeling that being closer to the sea air would be a refreshing change from the forested suburbs, we made our decision and began looking in areas across the river, over the Walt Whitman Bridge in the Garden State of New Jersey.

CHAPTER TWO

The Garden Variety

Richard still needed to drive into Philadelphia where he was working at a GE plant and so we needed to find a house within reasonable driving distance for his commute. We also wanted to continue to use Philadelphia as our source for entertainment and for socializing. We had arrived in the United States without much in the way of financial resources, which had been the main incentive and justification for leaving England because the Generous Electric Company were enticing Richard by offering to pay him three times as much as his salary back home. We looked in a number of areas in south Jersey before deciding, in the end, on an unusual choice.

In our on-going house hunting across the river, we discovered what a lovely bridge the Walt Whitman Bridge was. Bearing the name of such a powerful and influential figure in American literature, it soared, as did Whitman's words, spanning the Delaware river from Philadelphia to New Jersey, so high it was a thrill to drive over it, if not a little scary on a windy day when there was a slight but discernible sway. Built in the years between 1953 and 1957, it had seven lanes and was one of the largest suspension bridges on the East Coast. It was built in honor of Walt Whitman (1819–1892) because he had lived the last years of his life in the small, but now rundown town of Camden, on the New Jersey side, very close to the Delaware River.

Whitman was an abolitionist and a humanist and his most famous work, which was written over a lifetime, was the great collection of poetry called *Leaves of Grass*. This lifelong endeavor included the writings he composed during his time spent observing and assisting the wounded in the field hospitals during the horror of the Civil War. Among the poems in the collection are "Song of Myself" and his elegy to the assassinated president, Abraham Lincoln, "When Lilacs Last in the Dooryard Bloomed." His poetry praised nature and the individual human role in it, and like Emerson, it elevates the mind, spirit, and the human form, deeming all worthy of praise.

He is joined together with another great artist on permanent exhibit at the Pennsylvania Academy of Fine Arts where a wonderful oil portrait of him painted by the Philadelphian native Thomas Eakins (1844–1916), is in on permanent display. Eakins, "America's greatest, most uncompromising realist, dedicated his career to depicting the human figure in oil and in watercolor." The two men were friends and admired each other's great talent and they shared a devotion to individualism, humanism, and the outdoor life. This compelling portrait of Whitman was painted at his house in the river town of Camden not long before his death.

Once over the delightful Walt Whitman Bridge, South Jersey seemed to quickly descend and disintegrate into an awful mess of awkward, poorly planned highways, with the now easily recognizable, un-excusable, ugly black spaghetti power cables hanging messily overhead and teetering precariously on the over laden poles. One needed eyes in the back of the head to negotiate the pitfalls of making a left turn because you were expected to read ambiguous signs, which had already flashed passed you before you realized you were meant to turn into a right hand jug-handle, in order to make a left turn. Large and undisciplined traffic circles loomed before you and a free-for-all style of driving sometimes forced you into rotating the circle in a crazed state and to circumnavigate it several times before it was possible to disconnect at the desired exit and escape. Route 130 had many circuitous routes, all of them littered with a mish-mash of gas stations, junk food joints, flashy car dealerships, cheap tawdry strip malls, and seedy motels with indiscreet "sex shops" displaying a popular, sexually beckoning motive, the ever-lovable flashing dancing girl sign placed in the dirty window. It required a mindset of grim determination to drive through it all and to hopefully arrive, mostly unscathed, but shaky, sometime later, at the welcoming turn off which led to the attractive paths and grassy Parkway, which would bring us to the house we had chosen in the Garden State community that we would now called home.

    A planned community had been built that contained a stylish selection of affordable housing, nicely landscaped and set out in separate sections, which contained its own elementary schools, outdoor sports facilities including a large pool, which was open to families living in each of the planned sections throughout the summer holidays. There was also another feature that pleased us, an idea ahead of its time, the township boasted that the planned community would also be an integrated community and that a percentage of the homeowners would be from mixed races. It seemed a brave and revolutionary idea and felt like a breath of fresh air after the scared stiff and stuffy conservative community we had just left. It was exactly what we wanted for our children, a healthy, multi-racial living and learning environment that would fit them well for the world in which they lived. It might have been experimental but it was an experiment we gladly bought into, as did all the residents of Willingboro, New Jersey. But not quite all of them. A furor had started ten years previously when a statement was issued by the builder William Levitt who had other communities in New Jersey where he had established a "whites only" policy. He was afraid if one house was sold to a black family then no whites would buy his homes; so broad and rampant was racism at that time. But America was changing. Bill Levitt underestimated the power of the budding civil rights movement. He had missed the signs and was proposing to create a township "dedicated to the principle of segregation," a New Jersey attorney had accused. Into this hot mix stepped a retired army soldier who had served in Europe and had gone on to a second career as an equal opportunity officer with ITT Corporation; he was a civil rights leader and an ordained minister. When a Levitt sales agent told him "we don't sell to blacks," he filed a complaint with the state division against discrimination. A legal battle ensued and Levitt lost all appeals even his last-ditch effort to the US Supreme Court and finally announced a "voluntary" integration program. Willie James bought his house in Willingboro followed over the years by many more African Americans. He stated that he was not going to sneak around trying not to be seen—"Either people were going to accept us, or they weren't." On the whole people did accept Willie James and his family, which opened the door a little wider for other black families to come into the town and make the place their home.

 We bought a light and roomy four-bedroom colonial-style single house, which was attractive with shuttered windows and a modern kitchen and a good size front and back garden, a large cherry tree in the front and shade trees in the back, and it felt to us to be a pretty perfect purchase.

 Our street had lots of children playing together, and I found once again how open, friendly, and helpful Americans can be. Little girls came running over to say hello to Beth and to be little mothers to toddling Andrew. With the addition of several neighborhood children ever-present, and all playing wildly in our garden, we were not a quiet family and I sometimes felt sorry for our neighbors, a very quiet, dignified, church-going African American family next door. They treasured their garden, and it was manicured beautifully, with perfectly planned, planted, and cared for flower beds. Their polite and gracious teenage daughter with a beautiful smile never missed sending a cheerful daily greeting in our direction whenever she saw us. They often had to deal with the noise from our back garden (yard) as up to eight high-energy children from the neighborhood played vigorously with bats and balls and dolls, all the while yelling and laughing as they took turns hanging upside down from the backyard monkey bars. Our African American neighbors were very tolerant.

In London we had left behind a small, but first-owner new, two–bedroom town house in an attractive and interesting old town called Uxbridge, west of London, and as it happened, only about five miles away from William Penn's old family estate. My grandmother had left me a small amount of money in her will, which had helped with the purchase, and with some money left over, I bought some good and fashionable modern Scandinavian teak furniture. Other immigrants to the United States had brought furniture with them, but Richard was against the idea so, mad as hell, I had to sell all of my new furniture that was bought with my legacy before we left London. This meant I had to find something quickly for the family to sit on and something for them to sleep on in our New Jersey house. The problem was we didn't have enough money for new furniture so I was forced to be resourceful. Garage sales were a new experience for me, and at first, I had to swallow my pride as I was forced to rummage around other people's left-over stuff to furnish a four-bedroom house. I was really beginning to feel the "poor immigrant" experience. And then it became a challenge as I ventured to more affluent areas and found good stuff that I was comfortable in buying and living with. Another point occurred to me— I hoped to spend just a few years in America and to persuade Richard that this was only a temporary stay, so with that on my mind, it didn't matter that I was buying stuff in a garage sale. I could live with it; it wouldn't be for long. I furnished the entire four-bedroom house for $200 and boasted about it with reversed snobbery.

We had barely moved in and unpacked our few possessions from our cases and trunks and arranged the varied assortment of furniture, lamps, linens, dishes, and knick knacks I had picked up at garage sales, when we were able to join in an experience, which would be shared globally as the first of its kind in human history. An awe-inspiring event! The Apollo moon shot.

Among my garage sale finds was an ugly-looking television set. It was a console, a style that was popular in those days, but its outside fake wood surface had been streak stained with a very worrying color, which I can only describe as a muddy, blue brown. However it worked, in that on the black-and-white picture on a ten-inch screen, although slightly fuzzy from time to time, you could just about make out familiar features like a human head and body. It was far from perfect for the task we now demanded of it, but when it happened we were as full of wonder and disbelief, excitement, and exhilaration, and as tearfully amazed as anyone else on the planet. Sadly, the assassinated President Kennedy had not lived to see the culmination of his dream become an actual reality, and this made the event even more poignant. But the dedicated scientists and technicians had worked with an intense passion and devotion and overcame the enormous difficulty and, indeed, the odds, to get the job accomplished, and we were poised to watch history happen before our eyes, courtesy of my prized garage sale purchase, a $20 muddy- blue-brown, ten-inch console television set!

Work on this courageous, difficult, and dangerous, moon-shattering event began in earnest after President John F Kennedy's address to congress in 1961 where he declared his belief in a national goal of "landing a man on the moon" by the end of the decade. It would have been better perhaps to decide to do it exclusively for its scientific achievement, but the primary push behind it was to beat the then USSR in the competition for supremacy in space. This, of course, doesn't in the least diminish the incredible scientific accomplishment made by the National Aeronautics and Space Administration, but perhaps it should be remembered that there was also an urgent political push behind this conscientious effort. But better us than them.

And here we were, on July 20, 1969, waiting to watch history being made before our eyes, our little family gathered around our old-fashioned television set that had, in fact, come from a different age and time compared to the mind-boggling, cutting-edge scientific experiment we were about to witness. We pushed away the half fearful thought that something horrifying might happen, plans would go wrong, and tragedy would unfurl in front of the eyes of the whole world watching, but we willed with all our hearts the success of their mission, America's mission. As the news stations and their commentators drew us all collectively closer together in an effort to give a step-by-step account of the event we would hopefully witness, tension everywhere was palpable. Everyone watching this stupendous happening felt they were also part of this American dream. I widened the thought, believing that in embracing this arrival of mankind's foot print on such a far horizon, a planet outside of the earth's atmosphere, it would also be appropriate to say that "the world [including space], is my country and mankind my race!"

Our hearts were pounding as we watched in disbelief as a shadowy and fuzzy—was it the old television set—black and ghostly white picture blinked at us from the screen. There were tears in our eyes, for there before us was the shape of a man tentatively emerging from the capsule to the top of the ladder. He and his fellow astronaut had journeyed 250,000 miles through space from Earth for this moment, both backed by the culmination of years of work performed by the world's smartest scientists, all for this first, miraculous moment. A simple man dressed in a cumbersome silvery space suit and wearing a huge helmet looking too heavy for his head, his life dependent on the large square oxygen tank strapped to his back came into focus. One false move wouldn't bear thinking about as he gingerly stepped onto and made his way slowly, from the top of the ladder that extended down from the *Apollo* space capsule to the strange and scarily foreign surface of the moon below. The capsule looked precarious in the way in which it had landed, sitting on this weird, otherworldly, dusty gray, fluffy snowy, stony surface, etched in extreme and eerie contrast against the dense blackness of space.

Neil Armstrong was that man, and as he began his descent to the surface of the moon, he moved awkwardly, slowly, and with painful caution. His hesitant steps finally brought him to the bottom of the ladder where in a second his heavy-weighted space boot made its historic first step onto the lunar surface, followed by the inaudible but visual thud of the second boot. He was still standing upright; in fact, he skipped a few steps like an excited child finding himself in a new wonderland for the first time. And then he spoke these now immortal words: "That's one small step for man; one great leap for mankind." Tears and cheers of wonderment, relief, joy, and pride swept out across the population of the Earth, and in no lesser way from our own little family than from anywhere else on the planet.

Neil Armstrong and his fellow traveler in space, Buzz Aldrin, in their spectacularly successful journey from our Earth to the moon's surface had joined and achieved what scientists had been dreaming of for many hundreds perhaps thousands of years. Since before the time of Galileo and then of Newton and back even to the ancient Greeks, who named them as their gods, there have been star gazers, all speculating and longing for knowledge, which would bring them closer to understanding what to them were the heavens. Mapping the journey of the moon and the stars, watching and plotting the mysteries of the universe has been a human pre-occupation since the ancient Greeks and probably from earlier civilizations. The relief and pride felt by everyone connected with the project was palpable, and the noting of the significance of the scientific success of the mission was applauded around the world, and for weeks after the event we relived the amazing accomplishment by Neil Armstrong and Buzz Aldrin and their team. In unison the whole world cheered. It was a momentous occasion for all those lucky enough to witness it, one that the old would tell the young and those yet to be born—"I watched the first human step on to the moon's surface. He was an American!"

We settled easily into this community but again I felt like a curiosity for many people in Galton Lane, but I cannot fault a single one of my neighbors. On one occasion, while a gaggle of girls were watching me change Andrew's nappy or diaper, their giggling and pointing at his private bits prompted the inevitable question. What's it called? "A penis," I replied. This information went directly back into the home of five girls and it resulted in an upset mother calling to complain that I had used the word "penis" in front of them. "But that's its name. Why would you call it anything else?" I tried to explain, but the point seemed to be lost.

⁂

I also noticed that there was never any real, hard conversation among the neighbors about the Vietnam War that was raging nearly out of control in Indo China, until the battered boys began returning home and truth and reality fought face-to-face with the justification put out by the governments "political line." Without the benefit of information from the world class daily reporting

THE RELUCTANT IMMIGRANT

done by the British Broadcasting Corporation on radio and television, I pined for reliable, uncensored news. The miserable radio and television news and general programming offered in the United States bordered on being a nonsensical, a wasteland. Every channel was commercial, and every ten to fifteen minutes there was a commercial break. I thought that attention span here must have been seriously impeded as a result. Unfortunately much of this was happening before National Public Radio and PBS came along to give us weight, gravitas, and the balance I expected from informed journalism. We needed them now but they were not up and fully running until April 1971, just in time to be able to cover the US Senate hearings on the Vietnam War.

Even before we left England for the United States, there were many street demonstrations, which started in 1963, on both sides of the Atlantic against the American-led Vietnam War. But now in 1969, this country's young and more informed citizens were organizing on student campuses. This was a draft war and young men from all over the country were protesting and burning their draft cards in defiance. The casualty rate was very high and continued to climb. In all 2.59 million served; 1 in 10 men were killed. The average age was twenty-two years. And in total nearly 60, 000 young fighting men were killed.

Lyndon Baines Johnson, a Democrat from Texas, had the presidency forced upon him tragically, following the horrible assassination of President John F. Kennedy in Texas in 1963. He completed Kennedy's term and was then re-elected in his own right, winning by a large margin in the 1964 presidential election. Although his escalation of the Vietnam War was his eventual downfall, he started his presidency in a big way and was a great hero of the people. He was responsible for the "Great Society" legislation, which included laws that upheld Civil Rights, introduced Medicare, Medicaid, Environmental Protection, Aid to Education, War on Poverty, Public Broadcasting, Gun Control, the Voting Rights Act and the Space Race. A noble and necessary contribution to a modern society. Sadly, he listened too much to his generals and buckled under the weight of their frequent bad advice, forcing him into a corner where he might, as a Democratic, look weak if he didn't continue to pour more money and many more young American men into that hell-hole in Vietnam. The war dragged on, becoming more complicated almost daily, with casualties and deaths escalating enormously and the anti-war movement was becoming stronger and more influential among the young and particularly among the Democrats. Johnson's popularity steadily declined and his re-election bid collapsed as a result of the turmoil within the Democratic Party, which was a response to the fierce opposition in the country against continuing the Vietnam War.

The whole anti-war culture grew, and because of my ongoing interest in things political, I was drawn into the mix of demonstrations now held regularly in downtown Philadelphia at City Hall. "War is Unhealthy for Children and all Living Things" read a poster I bought at an anti-war rally in center city, which I hung in my daughter Beth's bedroom. Taking the children to anti-war demonstrations, Andrew in a pushchair or stroller and Beth waving a little American flag is not the best way for a new immigrant to behave. "We'll be deported," cried my anxious and angered husband. He had a point. "See if I care," I retorted. There was nearly a war on the home front! I continued to demonstrate and I was impressed with the courage and passion that brought people of all ages and from all walks of life together on these occasions, bumping against policemen or cops with truncheons, and of course, guns. They looked very serious but were not always threatening. "They will photograph you," Richard anguished. "I'll wear a longer skirt so I don't stand out and I'll fake an American accent," I replied. I wore large anti-war buttons on my clothes and bought bumper stickers for our car, but out of sympathy and

THE RELUCTANT IMMIGRANT

understanding for Richard's concerns and fear I might alienate my new neighbors or that we might be deported, I didn't stick them on the car or anywhere publically visible. You have to concede some things! I bought all the new 45 rpm records made by the musical stars of the public rebellion like Joan Baez and Pete Seeger, Peter, Paul, and Mary. "We Shall Overcome" became a rallying cry against the war along with a dozen other songs I can remember to this day and they inspired the courageous battle on the home front which raged, not always peacefully, but determinedly against the war in Vietnam through music and song. War is a sadness that seeps into the psyche and takes away the good taste of all things pure and beautiful, and a part of your mind is always in anguish over it! I was sure that an ongoing war had been fought somewhere on the earth since the day I was born, and I was disgusted. What is it about men? Perhaps we can blame too much testosterone in the air!

There existed in the Philadelphia/New Jersey area an English "old boy" network mostly centered around the English game of rugby, which was named after the establishment (posh and private) English school of the same name. The game has a history that goes back to 1750 but the rules of the game as they exist today were revised between 1859 and 1865. The boys of rugby school produced the first written rules for their version of the sport in 1870 based on the innovation of "running with the ball" set in place by the "Godfather" (my nick name) of the game, a man called William Webb Ellis. The game is now played all over the world especially in places that were once part of the old British Empire, as was another popular English sport, cricket. Rugby, however, carries the rather amusing, though unenviable quote, an old saying that I think still aptly applies—"Rugby is a game for barbarians played by gentlemen." My husband, Richard, played the game of rugby from the time he was a young boy until he was well past fifty years old, when he perhaps should have known better, and he bears all the scars to this day. The wife of a rugby player is called a "rugby widow," or she could also be called either really stupid or something mystical like a saint, and to some extent, it depends on your particular point of view. How you deal with a spouse who is absent from family duties being away at "practices" sometimes two evenings a week, who leaves on Saturday mornings and returns late at night inebriated and still wearing the same gear he wore twelve hours earlier, which is now covered in thick muck and mud, a spouse who then spends the remainder of the weekend recovering, complaining, and pampering his injuries as if they were genuine trophies, requires a determined and sometimes devious plan to counteract. To be an ardent "follower" of your husband and all the activities associated with this sport went against everything I wanted to do. I had my own passions and agenda, and so I made my own arrangements, and with like- minded rugby widows enjoyed instead the theatre, concerts, foreign movies, new restaurants, and arranged for baby sitters accordingly. The other thing I absolutely refused to do was wash the filthy, mud-caked, beer-stained, stinking rugby kit! Richard's mother, a lovely lady, had dutifully washed her son's kit since he was a boy and right up until, with visible relief, she handed her son over to me. I had the reputation among the male establishment as being "one of those women's libbers" and consequently Richard received considerable commiseration and consolation all of which he lapped up. However, one of my new, dearest, and stalwart friends and co-conspirators was Kathryn, and she and I had a great time on our own Saturday adventures, and by insisting on our independence on these occasions, we were able to remove any, or almost any, feelings of aggravation or resentment. These emotions would have undoubtedly surfaced and become a big problem if we had believed it "our duty" to wash dirty kit and drag ourselves and of course our kids around every weekend of the long season. At risk of spending too much time and space on this male-driven activity and obsession, I'll move on.

By this time one could not avoid recognizing the distressed look of a returning Vietnam soldier and a group of Philly players who lived in south Jersey decided to start a new rugby team and named it after a local river. It was called the Rancocas Valley Rugby Club. I became sympathetic to this cause because their intention was to encourage these sad, dazed young men and introduce them to the game of rugby and help them be part of the camaraderie it offered. Richard was asked to take on this challenge and coach this motley group of young men in their early twenties who had never heard of the game before and shape them into a team respectable enough to hold their own against other teams now cropping up in other states. I supported this and met many of these sad, strange, hairy, uncombed, gangly, and spaced-out young men and invited them into my home, where like a mother hen, I hoped to feed them and soothe some of their pain while also hoping that my own young but growing children wouldn't ask too many questions or one day emulate their behavior.

During the off rugby season months came glorious summer, and we discovered and reveled in the absolute joy of New Jersey's sea shore, commonly referred to simply as the shore. Even before the Atlantic City Expressway was built, which can now deliver you to the beach in less than one hour, you could drive across countryside and head for Island Beach State Park in about the same time. Richard had been correct on our first day excursion to the beach to take the small back roads where the soil was flat and sandy and the countryside was a delightful surprise, dotted with small vegetable and fruit farms with their fresh produce available cheaply at roadside stalls along the way. We drove through sleepy rundown villages, but it was pretty, very pretty, and there seemed to be something special about the light. We also discovered a massive lake that was full of colorful, bright red cranberries, millions of them. This unexpected place was where they were harvested, and it was a wonderful sight. As we drove closer to the sea or shore, a hazy, reflective brightness hung in the soft, slightly salty air, which was almost palpable, and you could feel that close proximity of our destination coming nearer, the salt being drawn and spread from that great mass of water, the Atlantic Ocean, by the breeze.

Before arriving at the beach we had to pass through a number of tacky townships, one after another running together and producing a disappointing contrast. They all wore an air of impermanence as if one good storm from the sea would blow the lot away. Small, cheap shacks passed for beach houses, then inevitably, farther along would be a similar structure but this would pass for a bar, although most people didn't pass the bar. They stepped right inside to cool off and to quench thirsts, and since they were open all hours, they were very popular watering holes. Even though the summer visitors were spending money in many ways in the community, there were still zoning laws everywhere, which were a nuisance and really just an excuse for the local law to slap a fine on your car since nowhere seemed to be approved for parking. You could be easily nabbed or caught by enthusiastic coppers or police lurking close to the popular beach crime scenes. I'd never heard of a privately owned beach. It seemed very undemocratic to me, so I thought it was an even bigger nerve to pay a charge for stepping foot on a particular townships' stretch of the beach with a "proof of payment" ink mark stamped somewhere on your body (hand actually) before you could feel the sand between your toes and sea spray on your face. So invariably we headed for the state park beach because it was well organized with the necessary facilities like changing rooms, toilets, or bathrooms and also with showers, food, and drink. Once on the beach all frazzle faded away. The beach was beautiful, wide and deep and soft and white. The sky was a cloudless blue and the magnificent Atlantic a deeper blue, boasting awesome and enormous wild rollers, wave after wave, a hypnotic, exciting, deafening, and exhilarating experience, which overwhelmingly trumped all the tack. The *sun*. Coming from a cold, windy, and often wet island in the North Sea with weather that was unpredictable at best in any season, we were just like all Brits—hungry for the sun's unrelenting and constant ability to pour therapeutic heat onto our pathetically wimpy and blindingly white bodies.

Fire hot, the sun burned down on us and we welcomed it like lost warriors who had finally found their way home. In England "quaint" medieval architecture was good, but we had an overabundance of it. We were tripping over so much of it; we were fed up with it always in our way— roads had to be built around it— disrupting the traffic. Although everybody loved having ancient memories in stone, it was always looking at us, begging for constant upkeep. And yes, it is true. Sometimes some frustrated, sacrilegious young Angles, often from past centuries, had added to the existing medieval graffiti by making a modern contribution of their own mark for posterity. But they are not really responsible; the fault of their bad behavior can be blamed on the English weather. They needed a distraction because they were so bored in their poor, chilly, and sunless state. The British nation would have collectively and gladly agreed to have half of the ancient "quaint" stuff transported to this new America, where it was in such very short supply, in exchange for some of their Sun.

Sunscreen was scoffed at almost unanimously in England, and burnt, red, skinning, pre-cancerous skin was part of our collective pact every summer. If you were lucky and put enough baby oil on your skin, you could get a good fry going, and after the slightly uncomfortable period called shedding, with the accompanying burning sensation, itching, and sleepless nights when even a single sheet could be a burden on the body, you emerged from it all with a hard-won tan, which could carry you on through to autumn or fall!

Legs, now tanned and glistening, emerged from under short-shorts and were shamelessly shown off with pride, the pride and power that comes with the new revolution for women. Woman had been supporting each other by flexing our fledgling "women's rights" muscles for quite a while, speaking up in situations where our mothers would have flinched away with embarrassment. But our own commonsense demands for equality were making waves through the turbulent, unchallenged ocean of sperm, but now, as a result of an amazing and seemingly long overdue scientific breakthrough, women also had the birth control pill! Armed and protected from here on, women could enjoy their sexual urges fully confident that they couldn't get knocked up or in the family way– or unknowingly impregnated unless we chose to on our very own terms! We felt like Amazon women with the power of the sun on the outside and the power of the pill on the inside; we were formidable! My soul mate Kathryn and I took it a step further.

We were often together and minding the five children we shared while our husbands were sailing, which was their new summertime "get away" sport. Sailing was a wonderful, worthy, new, and manly, get-away-from-it-all-especially- wives-and-children, day-long summer escape sport that our husbands now wholeheartedly embraced. Naturally we also felt the need to be engaged in a pastime equally challenging and rewarding. We needed our own sport, and naturally we chose the sport of mental aerobics. We had decided our bodies were doing just fine thanks to scientific progress, but we were somewhat worried about our minds, having the usual difficulty of holding and finishing a thought or sentence with a gang of kids constantly interrupting and demanding kid-like attention. We decided we needed an intellectual challenge and the usual book shop "soft summer romance reading" preferences didn't appeal to us. We needed something deeper, meaningful, and challenging, even shocking, something we could get our teeth into, and at my suggestion and without a whisper of hesitation, we dared each other to read a new and dangerously scary book published in 1968 by the great Soviet writer Aleksander Solzhenitsyn called *The First Circle*. Solzhenitsyn first wrote this book with ninety-six chapters but he worried that he wouldn't be able to get the book published in the then USSR, not only because of its content but because of its length, so mercifully for Kathryn and I, he produced a "lightened" version containing only eighty-seven chapters! It was all we had hoped for! Briefly, the novel, which is highly autobiographical, depicts the lives of the occupants of a *sharashka*, a bureau of gulag inmates located in the Moscow suburbs. Many of the prisoners were technicians or academics who had been arrested in Joe Stalin's purges, which followed the Second World War. These prisoners had some "privileges," meaning, that they were able to just about stay alive with small daily rations and reasonable work assignments, but the threat of being sent to a Siberian labor camp haunted them, and if they misbehaved or found any disfavor with their guards or keepers, off they went to the horror of the frozen steppe on Russia's most eastern wasteland from where no soul ever returned. Solzhenitsyn plucked the story line from Dante's first circle of "Hell in the Divine Comedy'—where non-Christians and philosophers of ancient Greece were allowed to live in a walled garden. Barred, because of their inconvenient birth date, they could not get into heaven because they were born before the birth of Christ so they had never been converted, very tricky, but they enjoyed a small space of freedom in the heart, and presumably heat, of the first circle of hell. As you can imagine, this book was a page turner. On a few occasions one of us would weaken with a pathetic "I can't go on" expression, but with stern encouragement from the other, we both finished that book, all eighty-seven chapters by the end of the summer and somehow all the children survived, no one drowned, and they probably thrived from the steadfast example we had set as a result of our determination to keep going when faced with a very difficult challenge.

The children were growing and thriving in their new environment. We were pleased with the schools and what they offered for their age group. Beth had lots of friends on Galton Lane, and the new children she met in school also became friends. The school pool was a great hit with every family and offered swimming lessons at an early age. Andrew could just about swim before he was four years old and was fearless in the water. Andrew was in preschool for only half a day, but I still tried to find unusual and challenging activities for them at home.

I loved the idea of painting to music and Richard made a large sturdy easel, which allowed for two kids to paint together on either side of the easel at the same time. Sometimes friends joined them, but when one of these children demonstrated in their own home by "throwing" paint without the use of an easel or any background music, a technique I taught them that was not overly popular with the child's parents. I was just as happy when my two were alone together because I could be more creative with them and they responded equally themselves by being more creative. I tracked down art supplies and used the large family room (nothing comparable in England) with its easy-to-clean flooring, placed large art paper on either side of the easel and put on my long playing record of Bach's Brandenburg concertos. My children were happy and creatively engaged for hours listening and painting at the same time and in rhythmic time to the music they were listening to, as each input propelled and stimulated the other.

This didn't make artists of them, but it did continue to develop their love and understanding of classical music and developed in both of them a good ear. They had been exposed since infancy to my song singing and to all the music from our large classical collection of LP records, which we had both insisted should accompany us across the ocean to be part of our new home, wherever that would be. Maybe they also inherited their musical inclination from their mother, grandmother, and grand aunt who had graduated from her studies in pianoforte from the London College of Music at the young age of fifteen years. My mother had also always played the piano from a very young age and the sisters performed regularly together at musical soirees in the area of south London where they were brought up. I had long understood the advantages of early music education and thought that Beth was at just the right age to become involved. After much inquiry and research I was fortunate to find what I wanted in a small town called Medford, quite quaint, which was a half an hour drive southeast from our town, along small country roads.

The Medford Music School functioned in a large old

wooden house that was full of quirky character, so I loved it. They offered a two-year course in early childhood music education with emphasis on keyboard, created by the Japanese company Yamaha and called the Yamaha Preparatory Course for Piano. They, of course, make beautiful pianos but also, oddly, they manufactured motor bikes! They stood in competition with the other Japanese company called Suzuki, which offered at that time a better-known music program for young children, but for the violin. The Suzuki Company also manufactured motor bikes! My mind was in a boggle! The corporate idea behind the Yamaha program was, of course, to train and teach music to children at an age when their minds were at their most open to new ideas. The curriculum included notation, reading music using small black magnetic notes that could be easily moved around a music staff (lines and spaces). This enabled children to learn the names of the lines and spaces, in both bass and treble clef. They were taught the fundamentals of rhythm with percussive instruments and worked from a beautifully illustrated and creative book that was fun to work with while helping to reinforce the teachers' instruction. Essentially this made learning fun and that way the children remained enthusiastic and engaged and it made competition among the children easy and acceptable and healthy.

I was so impressed with the whole program that I was given a job of selling it to interested parents. Sometimes I would organize an interested group within my wide territory, and by putting some passion along with knowledge on the subject into my sales pitch, more parents signed up. I believed in the program and saw the results not only with Beth and other children but later with Andrew. Many parents would like their young children to have piano lessons, but without sufficient musical background the young child is inevitably overwhelmed by the task, having to overcome such an enormous amount of technical and musical information before their little fingers could play anything remotely musical. Ninety percent of them dropped out within the first year and remain bored and hostile to the idea of learning an instrument from then on. One great outcome from my employment association with the school was that I was entitled to purchase a Yamaha piano at the wholesale price. I chose the least expensive because even with this incentive, it took all my paychecks to eventually pay for it. But now we were ready to put the Yamaha program into practice; both Beth and Andrew had a piano to play.

My own involvement and connection with this organization and the Medford School of Music began to open many doors for me, and my own passion and musical pursuit began to take form. I began voice lessons and soon realized from my background and training in London and my membership in a fine choral society there, that I was ready to join a decent choral group. I was told that the New Jersey Glassboro State College Choir were looking for voices to swell their numbers for an upcoming performance of Verdi's Requiem, a massive composition that I had always loved but had never had the chance to perform. I was so excited at the prospect of singing this enormous and glorious music I practically floated through the audition with great ease. It is a stunningly powerful, difficult, and dramatic piece and among the great favorites of the choral repertoire. When Verdi's friend Alessandro Manzoni, the Italian writer and humanist, died in 1873, Verdi resolved to write a Requiem mass for him. It was originally named the Manzoni Requiem, and throughout the work, Verdi uses vigorous rhythms, sublime melodies, and dramatic contrasts the most recognizable of these being the electrifying Dies Irae, which crops up like a terrifying exclamation mark throughout the work. It's even frightening to sing! It was also wonderful to be singing again and I loved every rehearsal and performance; the whole experience was exhilarating.

From this experience I was recommended to audition for

the Rutgers University Choir, New Jersey's acclaimed state university, which was in New Brunswick, very close to New York. Again I sailed through the audition and was excited that our conductor was an up-and-coming young man called Michael Tilson-Thomas. We rehearsed on campus and the oratorio we were to sing and perform was an obscure composition by an American composer I had never heard of, and I was not alone. His name was Horatio Parker, and the piece was called Hova Novissima. It was composed in 1892 and was performed widely in America and in England where it received much acclaim even achieving the honor of performing at the prestigious English music festival called the Three Choirs Festival. Not being performed much today, our conductor Maestro Tilson-Thomas wanted to reacquaint audiences with the composition. Our maestro was so energetic in his passion for the music and conducting in general and with this piece in particular that on more than one occasion he leapt so high on the podium that he actually fell off! His acrobatics were a highlight of all our rehearsals and kept us trying to control our mirth, hiding our giggles behind our scores. We performed the piece in a rave performance in Carnegie Hall in New York City and there followed other equally challenging concerts by more traditional composers. Maestro Tilson-Thomas rose to become one of the world's most respected and famous conductors and teachers and now leads his own orchestra, the New World Symphony, in a new, exciting state-of-the-art concert hall built for him by the eclectic architect Frank Gehry and located in the heart of downtown Miami in Florida. I was happy, hooked, and hungry for more. In my teens I had been the school soprano soloist, and at age eleven was the "chosen one" from my elementary school to sing in the London Schools Choir at the Royal Albert Hall in celebration of the Festival of Britain in 1951. I had to sing!

News from home had been worrying for some time. The

English of my parents' generation were often tight-lipped over health issues, and my father had unhappily been diagnosed with Alzheimer's disease in his late sixties. But at that time, with little or no advice or information regarding the disease and few treatments readily available, both my mother and my sister were naturally distraught as to how best to help him. This is long before some of the help and information that is available today. Basically, like it still is today, it was up to the family to watch out for their loved one, which is a daunting responsibility under any circumstances. Having moved some years earlier from the family home, which was larger and had a big garden, it was perhaps, fortunate that my parents now lived in a townhouse community served by good public transportation, shops, and a park just a few minutes away so they were not isolated, which would have been worse. Everyone in England has their local pub within walking distance and that is where my dear dad would wander, often in his carpet slippers, at the early hour of eight o'clock in the morning. The cleaners would also be there attending to their chores along with the owners of the establishment. He was a regular at the King's Head and they understood and would even pull him a pint of beer and place it down beside him at his usual table. But he never drank one sip. He just sat there. This was routine, and by this time the owners had called my mother who would rush along to bring him home. He also got into the habit of calling my mother "Patty," which he had occasionally called me, and sometimes in the middle of the night, my mother would be woken by energetic sounds from the kitchen as he was trying to make tea, cold tea, using every cup, saucer, jug, and container he could find. There seemed nothing anyone could do except to try and avoid him hurting himself. I think my mother kept a great deal from me to save me from the worry, which would have had me jumping on a plane to London every month to help share some of the burden.

The situation was deteriorating and I was making arrangements to have Beth and Andrew looked after by some of my kind neighbors when I got the call. It was early in the morning of October 24, 1975, and I was still in bed when in the distance I heard the phone ring and Richard pick it up. I could tell from his tone, even in my sleepy state, that something had happened, and he walked gravely into the bedroom handing me the telephone. My darling father was dead. He was seventy years old. He had died of a massive stroke a few hours earlier. Now the children were awake and crying and trying to comfort me in their sweet way without understanding the gravity of the situation. They just knew that the grandfather they sadly never knew had just died at his home in London, and sadly, even though they hardly knew him, they wept for me.

The journey home seemed interminable and what I found when I arrived was worse. Understandable, but harsh criticism and incriminations came from my sister, blaming me for not having been there during his illness. She was right. I couldn't deny it and I understood her distress but I had had no control over the situation, and my own grief was so deep I didn't think I would ever recover. Fear and abject grief also came from my mother who clearly had been trying to keep going for so long by herself, feeling utterly alone in her own despair. I felt bereft and useless and ashamed and guilty. The funeral was a rainy blur, held in the dismal auditorium of the local crematorium. Quite a number of notable people in the newspaper world came to pay their respects, a good few of them journalist colleagues, also friends attended and relatives and neighbors, but the "reception" with the beer and gin and tonic (no ice) and the hastily made ham-and-cheese sandwiches, was commonly held in the home of the deceased. Mostly people stayed for a short and respectable time, but my father's family, the Garsides were a theatrical gang by profession and also liked a stiff scotch whisky to give them fortitude at a time like this, and they stayed on and on and it began to resemble a wake.

All members of the Garside family were a list of characters, having all descended from a long line of actors, many of whom had been famous Shakespearean actors in the eighteenth and nineteenth centuries. They liked a stage and my father's funeral gave them one.

My uncle Ron, always the "lad" and odd one out in the family of eight kids, dared to sit in my father's favorite chair, reminiscing and laughing as his grief turned to almost gleeful relief–Ha, my number wasn't up! As he raised the large beer he was drinking from Fred's favorite glass-bottomed, pewter beer mug, to drink to his brother's life and hopefully his afterlife, the bottom of the mug broke and fell out crashing completely to the floor, smashing and drenching him all over with a large full pint of best English bitter. There was a long worrying silence, my uncle Ron turned a soggy ashen gray before the mood of terror was broken and tentative laughter turned hysterical. My dad, Frederick Homer Garside, had certainly had the last laugh, and we could all hear his chuckle and see him winking his eye, wagging his finger at his wayward brother and grinning widely with his happy, gappy grin.

I returned back to my home on Galton Lane to discover that the house had been sold in my absence. To be fair to Richard, there had been some talk about a transfer to some unpronounceable little town in upstate New York, but it didn't seem imminent to me, and perhaps I pushed any idea of another move as far from my mind as possible. I felt as though I had just got a life together again in New Jersey, and I refused to leave another life behind.

The seven years spent in New Jersey were on the whole happy years, a period where we as a family found stability and growth. The children did well. We had all thrived and there was still a sense of pride in the success of our planned community. We explored the whole state of New Jersey, which was physically different in the north, which had hills and forests and perhaps being closer to New York, more sophistication than the sandy south. But we loved being close to the sea, which never disappointed, where the waves were exciting, the sand soft, and for the first time in my life, I was tanned pretty much all over and my most essential possession was a pair of sunglasses! We discovered sailing in the bright blue days, and lazing through the long warm nights, the children squealing with delight as they danced barefoot on the grass catching fireflies in the gathering dusk. We had neighborly competitions growing tomatoes, weighing them, and gave prizes for the biggest and the best. Then driving home from the shore, hot and sticky from the remnants of melted ice cream, with salt and sand stuck in our hair, skin beginning to burn, we would stop at the road stands for freshly squeezed fruit drinks and buy from a collection of different fruit, berries and iced watermelon and I wondered no longer why New Jersey was called the Garden State.

CHAPTER THREE

The City that Lights and Hauls the World

The decision to sell our house in New Jersey had been made while I was away in London, dealing with my own and my family's grief. In fact, I felt I had been conveniently out of the way. I know it was not deliberate, but it always seemed that way to me. I was understandably exceedingly upset and even angry.

Where on earth was this new, horrible place in the middle of nowhere, and how could you being to pronounce its ridiculous name? How could you even spell it if you wanted to? Why would you want to? I didn't care that a light bulb had flashed on in Thomas Edison's head and he had felt compelled to get off the train and to start a business in this dowdy town, immediately. Were there no other alternatives? What was the attraction? And what were the Dutch doing wandering around in the wilderness in 1609, so far from the sea and civilization, that they also thought it was a good place to pitch their tent? There are, of course, many very reasonable and historically legitimate reasons for all these decisions, but from my point of view, at that particular moment in time, they were all irrelevant. All I knew was that the winters were interminably long and known to be wickedly cold, dismal, and abysmal, with six months of below freezing cold temperatures and with ice and snow up to your ears. I would probably freeze to death! I refused to go. I hated Schenectady before I even set foot in the place. However, once again, full of anguish and hurt, I blindly groped my way through the motions of packing up a home, robotically forcing myself to get through the miserable ordeal, keeping myself silent for fear of an uncontrollable emotional eruption.

Rushing immediately on arrival to find somewhere suitable to live, being forced to pick a pokey house from a dismal selection but a house in the right school district, I plotted revenge every step of the way and kept muttering under my breath that this sacrifice had better lead to some enormous reward sometime soon. More importantly, where was I going to sing?

In truth, of course, it was not Richard's fault, although I wrongly felt that it was at the time, but I also realized that jobs in Philadelphia were shifting away and that the plant there was going to close down. He had been noticed for his smarts and been offered a chance to join the General Electric's prestigious 'think tank' in the Research and Development community, all of which was really a better fit for him than his previous position. The problem was its location. For me life felt like a continuing culture shock.

As with most things in life, once you give it half a chance, a bad idea can be softened around the edges and an, albeit, half or maybe even less than half acceptance could be possible, I emphasize the word *could*, might or maybe. This was not, however, immediately evident to me in Schenectady, in upstate New York.

To emphasize the point, if I tell you that a notice on the local cemetery gate states that if your beloved has the misfortune of falling off his or her perch after a certain date late in the year, burial will have to be in the spring. That's because the ground is frozen solid and it is impossible to dig a grave. Even if you have the need, you will also have a problem with burial before the ground freezes solid because you have to wait for the cemetery personnel to set light to a bundle of straw, designed for the purpose, then the straw will be placed on the gravesite and left to smolder for a day or so in order to melt the ice crystals and soften up the ground sufficiently for a shovel to be applied and a hole dug. It was always a disconcerting sight when driving along the road past the large cemetery, while in the middle of humming a comforting tune, to see eerie gray smoke swirling in heaven's direction coming from a melting job that was in progress on a well-chosen plot for a burial at the end of the week. Trespassing here was strictly off limits at Halloween!

However, still feeling my way around, I began to find out some interesting facts about Schenectady, New York. In many ways it didn't have to hide its little light bulb under a bushel; there was much for it to boast about. It is true, or "gospel" folk law, that the great light bulb in Thomas Edison's head did grow hotter the closer he came on the train to Schenectady, because the wise man had already done his research and that made all the difference to his decision. He got off the train in Schenectady because he already knew it was a great place to transfer his existing business, the Edison Electric Company, and in 1892 our generous benefactor named his new company the General Electric Company. There was already the American Locomotive Company in the town and the surrounding area was bustling with commercial promise, helping to make the place an important magnet for the new industrialists. In the nineteenth century, Schenectady was firmly on the map as a new center for industrial enterprise, and as an essential part of the equation, it also became an important transportation center when the Hudson River was connected to the Mohawk Valley and the great Lakes. In fact, the city was once known as "The City that Lights and Hauls the World."

However, by the time we arrived in 1976, GE's large plant was already in trouble, and an air of industrial decay hung over the town, its shops in the downtown area looked tired and dismal with that inevitable expression of desperately trying to hold on. The town wandered wearily but bravely through this period, painting a new face on store fronts here and there, but in general, it was just keeping afloat.

As I peered deeper I saw a tough town and a strong population who had the fortitude to hang together during the difficult down times, and there was enough money circulating from other good sources in different areas to make it viable. But the extreme winter climate was torture for me and I shivered all the time and tried to hibernate as much as I could every winter.

Schenectady was closely positioned to be near to the infamous snow belt, which meant it started snowing in November and continued snowing, with few letups, until late March and even April. The temperatures frequently plummeted down to the teens and even single digits, where they lingered for days, so that every new fall of snow froze immediately on top of the already existing layers of solid frozen snow. But if you were a native of this area, it was all you knew and you welcomed the first frost and flake with enthusiasm, dusting off skates and skis, sharpening their edges in anticipation for robust activity in the out of doors. Trying to fit into the general odd gaiety that the natives of these cold climes exhibited at this time of year, at the beginning of our first winter, Richard took the garden hose, before it also froze, and hosed a section of our large front garden where it immediately became the favorite neighborhood skating rink. I was horrified to see a large gathering of local lads, my son Andrew included, playing fierce games of fear-free hockey with the clashing glee of hockey sticks making sparks in the thin and frigged air while the dainty giggling girls in their bobbly hats and with their pretty white figure skates pirouetted and made figures of eight with grace and nonchalance completely indifferent to the boys, although they were only inches from each other. Never once was there an accident or a frantic call of complaint from a child's mother crying or threatening to sue because one of their dear children now had only one eye!

One of my problems was that I had never lived in a small town before, having been lucky to enjoy the easy stimulation, variety, and abundance of large city life, and I found the town claustrophobic, and not in the lease bit quaint. I would discover that the things I needed were there but you had to seek them out, for they were solitary; one concert hall which doubled as a theatre and one or two really good restaurants seemed at first sight all that was available. Another problem for me was a genuine feeling of agoraphobia—I had never lived so far from the sea before! In England the farthest point you can be from the sea is seventy miles. But what was beyond this small town and its limits would soon surprise me—I had yet to explore them.

General Electric's Research and Development Center was quite separate from the downtown plant and was situated in an almost suburban area called Niskayuna. At that time it employed approximately eight hundred PhDs who had come from all over the world to do research work, and so it was a very interesting international mix of the brightest and the best. Many of them were from Europe and a large number came from England. This, of course, changed the whole cultural climate and opened up a variety of opportunities as we were taken under many "wings" and shown aspects of the town that helped to slowly change my attitude, but that didn't happen overnight; it took considerable time. Nevertheless it was a relief to be connected to people from other places who themselves had been through the same culture shock and had emerged intact and with a healthy attitude about the town they now lived in. For many it was the attractions that lay beyond the town limits that gave enrichment to their lives, and we were pointed in that direction, finding big and welcomed surprises. We were soon making friends and found that a warm, welcoming social life thrived behind the banks of snow, but while commiserating with us for being so far from home, our new friends also reassured us that we were not, in fact, at the end of the world or even in Siberia, only in Schenectady, located in upstate New York, and there was a good and interesting life to be experienced with a lot of fun thrown in.

Since coming to America, however, I had lived my life aware of a great tugging perplexity within. Wanting, on the one hand, to walk away, as in a state of almost total denial, while at the same time being intrigued by the similarities but differences of language and of behavior, which made me want and need to give each new place some grounding and historical perspective, mostly for my own but also for my family's benefit. So when a puzzling question arose as to why there was such a variety of unusual names and spelling, why people spoke in a different way using consonants and vowels that sounded strange to my ear, or sang familiar melodies with unfamiliar words, and where puzzling local and national history was taught, unfamiliar holidays celebrated, it was essential to continue doing research, which gave me some reasonable knowledge of the bewildering newness I was surrounded by. With time this helped me bridge the gap toward assimilation and acceptance. I inevitably became interested enough in this new place to gather and dissect the complicated facts about its history, and gradually my attitudes and expectations changed even though as I peeled back the pages of its history I discovered how extremely complicated, while on another level, how familiar their early beginnings were. I am not trying to present a history seminar in my story, however, due to the English history taught to us in school in the fifties, I learned much about the ruling of the ranting and sometimes raving English royals over a period of a thousand years, a period of development that could be described as having made "two steps forward and one step back" with "civilization" shuffling along, carrying a ball and chain around its ankle for many centuries. Perhaps deliberately, but certainly due to the decisions made back in the early fifties by the British Board of Education, we were never introduced to early American history, and although I was well schooled, we passed only blithely over the American War of Independence—perhaps it was due to national denial of losing the colonies, and still a grudging sore spot for the establishment—so I knew little history of the "new world" or about any of the areas in which I was going to live before our arrival, but which now I was here felt, compelled, regardless, to address.

The native Indians had very deep roots in the area having lived there for centuries. The various tribes growing and trading together but also fighting frequently among themselves for control of the fertile land and access to the rich rivers, but they finally formed a confederation of five tribes who spoke Iroquois, the powerful Mohawks and the Oneidas, Onondagas, Cayugas, Senecas calling themselves the Mohawk Nation of the Iroquois

Confederation. Meanwhile the Dutch and other Europeans where flexing to spread out onto the brave new continent for mostly commercial reasons, but also for civic and religious liberty, depending how you frame the events.

The year 1609 was a memorable year for it brought the earliest European settlers from the Netherlands, then comprising what is now Holland and Belgium, to this region. Henry Hudson, the English navigator who happened to be in the employ of the Dutch East India Company, discovered the river that now bears his name, and he sailed approximately 150 miles north from New York, taking possession of the territory and held it in the name of the States- General of Holland. To the territory that they had acquired, the Dutch gave the name of New Netherlands.

The historical backdrop for much of this activity derives from the frequent and often bloody exchanges of the European "royal guard" as most of these countries were always jockeying and trumping and battling each other for power and influence within the European states and beyond, with their big eyes firmly fixed on the new empty American continent. This continuous political power play in the Netherlands, England, and France during this period lasted for many decades. In the land of the Iroquois Confederation, borders were fiercely fought over to gain territory and the subsequent skirmishes broadened to spill over into full-scale battles for territory among the tribes. Changes of allegiance and of fortune from all sides also added to the complications over the ownership of land among the multiple parties in play for the spoils.

The early history of Schenectady County is closely interwoven with that of the native Indians, chief among them being the Algonquin and the Iroquois, the latter being distinguished for their intelligence and warlike tendencies. In the contests waged by the rival European nations for the possession of the new country, the Iroquois were hostile to the French, but friendly to the

Dutch and the English. In 1618 they made a peace treaty with the Dutch, which was long and faithfully observed on both sides. The Dutch, as with all their European neighbors, were always intent upon commercial advantage, traffic, and gain, and being the first to arrive, they secured the rich fur trade from the native tribes, and in exchange for the furs, they gave the Indians trinkets, alcohol (fire-water), and firearms, which became a lethal combination for the tribes, but is about what you might expect from the Europeans if your objective is to undermine and take advantage of a fierce but "uncivilized" opponent who knew no better.

The name "Schenectady" or Schau-naugh-ta-da is not Dutch but is derived loosely from the language of the Iroquois Indian word that signifies for "over the pine plains" or "across the pines" and is said originally to have been used by them to designate Fort Orange, now the city of Albany, the state capitol, which is about fifteen miles south east of present-day Schenectady. Just to make it more confusing, this name was later used by the Dutch settlers, who reversed the original translation so the name then referred to the bend in the Mohawk River where Schenectady city lies today. Ever heard of Double Dutch? The Dutch were the first European colonists to arrive and settle in the area in 1661, and at that time, Schenectady was still part of the land that belonged to the Mohawk Nation of the Iroquois-speaking confederacy. The confederacy had been a "sophisticated society" of approximately 5,500 people, but had a continuing state of war over a period of thirty years first within the Indian tribes themselves then followed by the Dutch and the English and later still, the French, all of whom brought with them not only weapons and alcohol but diseases like small pox, measles, influenza, and lung infections, which contributed to the frequent decimation of the native Indian population.

To make sure the population of the tribes was maintained, the Indians had a practice of replacing those who had died from disease or violence by "adopting outsiders." This meant taking by force other men and sometimes women from different tribes along with European settlers to build up their numbers and replenish their ranks. The history of the region is long, and bloody but given the glorious bounty to be had on the new American continent, it isn't surprising that the Europeans fought furiously over the land grabs, assuring that the wars would be continuous for many decades to come, leaving populations demoralized and utterly exhausted at the end. It is what nations have always done across the globe and still continue to do.

Having used the winter by making the effort to understand some of the history of the area, it was with a more enlightened attitude that I was ready and able to actually explore it. When the ice and snow slowly but finally melted away, we congratulated ourselves at having made it through the longest and most harrowing winter in our memory. Our first spring arrived tentatively at first, and a sudden raw chill of wind could still catch at the throat and play annoyingly with our emotions until it gradually settled into something we could all recognize and agree upon, that the weather now resembled how we remembered spring should be. Away went the heavy multiple layers of essential inner and outer wear, and like small animals coming out of hibernation, we used our nose to sniff the degree of warmth in the clean air, agreeing at last that it was safe to wear a lighter sweater. Realizing that we should not waste the short summer ahead of us, we were determined to get as much out of the four warm months stretching in front of us as possible, and so we made every effort to explore the many beautiful areas outside of Schenectady.

We made an investment that would have an impact and play a large part in our lives for many years to come. We bought a boat. Our first boat was a twenty-four foot O'Day sail boat and ideal for the waters of the great Lake George, which was about an hour's drive north of Schenectady. It was large enough to sleep the four of us, but because there were so many lovely islands dotted about the pristine lake, it was also possible to tie up at a small dock, gather kindling and cook over a small fire, and camp overnight—which the children loved to do, while I preferred the small but comparative luxury of a berth. To our delight and surprise the lake water was completely clean and safe to drink, which we did on every trip, being thankful that the authorities of New York State had been so bold in their care of the great lake and had put into place every known environmental safeguard.

We called our boat *Meantime,* as in the "meantime they went sailing for nothing better to do." Back in London my sister had used the same name for her restaurant whose prestigious address placed it twenty feet from the old Cutty Sark schooner in the Royal Borough of Greenwich and the Greenwich Meantime. As I previously mentioned, Greenwich also boasts the beautiful Queen's House, one of Elizabeth I many dwellings along the Thames. But back in New York State, we had been delighted to discover our close proximity to the Adirondacks and Lake George and their long and important history. The whole area is very beautiful, but it is also a sad stage, where many monuments have been placed over the centuries, marking the spot where ugly battles raged, again involving the native Indians, the new Americans, and European armies and settlers. The area with the beautiful backdrop had also been a killing field and demanded the recognition of later generations to acknowledge the sacrifice and the need to commemorate the many thousands of lives lost in the attempt to possess the hills and valleys, the great lakes, and their idyllic banks.

Exploring the region on one occasion we drove to Fort Ticonderoga and unexpectedly discovered a small cemetery tucked away quietly on the grassy banks of the other great lake in the Adirondacks, Lake Chaplain— the waterway to Canada. The names of the very young soldiers, still visible on the worn down headstones, were all Scottish and contained the remains of an entire Scottish regiment from the Black Watch who were slaughtered fighting the French during the French-Indian wars. They now rest in this poignant place overlooking the beautiful Lake Champlain. The deaths of these soldiers so long ago still runs deep in the Scottish psyche, and to this day, the Scots have a battle cry—"Remember Ticonderoga," which they display with passion at various sporting events in the hope of undermining their opponents' prowess by putting the fear of God into them.

An earlier and more idyllic description of the area was written by Thomas Jefferson: "Lake George is without comparison, the most beautiful water I ever saw, formed by a contour of mountains into a basin 35 miles long and from 2–4 miles broad, finely interspersed with islands, its water limpid as crystal and the mountain sides covered with rich groves of silver fir, white pine, aspen and paper birch down to the water, here and there precipices of rock to checker the scene and save it from monotony. An abundance of speckled trout, salmon trout, bass and other fish with which it is stored, have added to our other amusements the sport of taking them."

Fortunately the summers, although short, were beautiful, warm, and sunny during the days and cool in the evenings, perfect for outdoor activities. Being a "chilly morsel" as my mother used to call me, I have to confess to preferring the sizzling heat of the New Jersey summers, but the air in Schenectady had a delicious quality to it like a glass of clean, cool, pure spring water. The climate was perfect for roses, and to my delight, there was an English rose garden in a park near the center of town. It seemed extraordinary to me that some small group or individual had either loved roses so much or missed England so much that they had been driven to create such a beautiful spot; it was my little retreat and it delighted me.

But that was not all. It had not been done without thought and planning. The park was called Central Park for a reason—its architect and designer was Frederick Law Olmstead who had been the creator of New York City's famous Central Park. In Schenectady, the land was chosen for its location. Being the highest elevation point in the city, it was a jewel in its own right and was approved for purchase by a group of civic-minded people from Schenectady who made up the Common Council in 1913. Olmstead's smaller Central Park with its acclaimed rose garden, Iroquois Lake, and a stadium tennis court was rightly treasured by the inhabitants of this small industrial town and that included me, for now.

Union College is a liberal arts college surrounded by eight acres of formal gardens and woodland. It is situated on the "nice" part of town close to what is still referred to as the GE plot, which was built for General Electric's executives in the nineteenth century who were lucky enough to find themselves with lots of money, which allowed them to be overly ostentatious in their choice of period building styles. They built grand houses next to each other, in what must have been a fierce competition for the biggest and the best.

Union College, having been founded in 1795, is claimed to be the oldest "planned" college in the United States. Reading an article that appeared in the *New York Times* in 2010, it seems it also had a working "plan" to avoid taking the visiting prospective students to the areas of downtown Schenectady because it was so rundown and unattractive that it was a real and definite put-off and most of them walked away saying "no, thank you." Although the college and the wider community seem to have improved their relationship, it had been laughably prickly since the college's founding in 1795. In 1832 a student wrote in his diary that the city was "only fit for hogs and Dutchman" and wondered "why the ways and walks were never cleaned, why never repaired?" He then exclaimed, "Oh, what a world of filth!" I have previously referred to the town's disappointing and dilapidated appearance, although I believe my view of it had to have been considerably better than in 1832. I do, however, rest my case on the subject.

The big question was why would a large world-class wealthy corporation like General Electric allow its famous home base town to become so rundown and become the butt of jokes everywhere—but people gazed into space with glazed eyes when I asked this question and I never got an answer.

Nevertheless, for better or worse, I had to live here and so wanted to be optimistic and was looking for redeeming features, and Union College could boast a particularly good one for me. Schenectady seemed to be a halfway stop between New York and Montreal, and there were often touring orchestras, theatre productions, and speakers who came and graced us with their talent for an hour or two before they flew away like little birds in the night to a tastier destination. Every month, a visiting chamber orchestra or solo instrumentalist would stop by and give a concert in the sixteen–sided Nott Memorial Hall built in 1875 on the Union College campus, and those events saved my life. I remember the fleeting visit of the great American composer Aaron Copland, whom I had admired for many years and who's whimsical and sometimes poignant American music touched and delighted me. He came to give a lecture and played selections of his piano music during a lunchtime recital appearance. My son, Andrew, a budding young pianist himself, was at home recovering from an ailment and was eager to accompany me to this special event. I was very excited on another occasion when the highly renowned English Chamber Orchestra, regarded as the very best orchestra of its kind in England, were billed to give a performance in Schenectady and a famous and dear old friend who played first horn with the ECO was going to be touring with them. I invited James to dinner before the performance and he regaled all of us with funny stories of the hectic touring schedule and his crazy international musical life. As he was leaving, he took me aside and asked me what on earth I was doing here in this "funny little town, come back to London where the real action is," he whispered as he left to delight the eagerly awaiting audience.

As in the other places I had lived in the United States most of the friends we made were not neighbors, although they were gracious and helpful at all times. We made our eclectic group of friends through the people Richard worked with at the R&D Center. Many of the wives were in the same position I was in and we were all there to help each other. They were a mixed international group and among them were Americans from other states, European's from the west and the east, and also Indians and Canadians. The Brits were the quickest to take us in and swarmed over us, delighted to have two more to add to the English group, and lifelong friendships were made practically overnight. There were many hilarious dinner parties and any occasion seemed to be a good excuse to get together. Those weekly events kept me laughing instead of crying, although I could see that it was easier for those Brits who had originally come from small English towns themselves to assimilate and settle more comfortably than I could in this small American town. Their expectations were not as high since they had not experienced the buzz of living in a large capital city like London, in fact in some ways they were overwhelmed by the constant stimulation of big city life and felt at greater ease in a town of manageable size. However, jokes and teases of every kind peppered our dinner conversations, and often as we dissected our lobsters, we cried with laughter into our bibs and nearly chocked from hearing the explicit details of some outrageously inappropriate dinner conversation!

The year of 1978 was to prove very difficult and challenging. Returning to the house on Westholm Road by car one bitter Saturday morning, I was met in the driveway by an anguished-looking Richard and alarmed children running to my side the moment I stopped the car. I tried to read their faces, but in an instant, I knew there was bad news from England. I had one younger sister who was born in 1945, but I had this dear brother/cousin who joined our family when his own mother, my mother's dearest sister, died suddenly and unexpectedly at a very young age, in the same year that I was born, 1940. My mother's sister had died after surgery, leaving her son, two-year-old Daniel alone, his father being away in the war and so my mother adopted him as her son and he was brought up in our family for many years as my brother. We were two years apart and very close, sharing the nightmares of many bombings, by comforting each other during those air raids along with our teddy bears in the sometimes "safe" cupboard under the stairs. When a warning of a heavier bombardment was expected, we went outside into the dreaded cold and damp Anderson shelter, which were built for most Londoners who had some available space around their house, by the London County Council. As an adult Danny had lived with his wife and family in Princeton for a period while we were also in New Jersey, and our families frequently socialized. Later, whenever he travelled in the States he went out of his way to visit me, the last time being four months earlier when he arrived with his handsome face, Irish eyes, chip-toothed grin, and the largest bowl of yellow chrysanthemums I had ever seen. I commented that he had "brought the warmth of the sun" into my winter house. The awful news that Danny had just died of a massive heart attack at the tragic young age of forty-two was almost too much to bear. Devastated, my own heart went cold with grief and outrage as I tried to grasp the shock of his death and the cruel reality that I couldn't financially justify a trip back to England for the funeral.

My mother had visited only a few months earlier and having her with me was a joy and her visit had been successful in many ways, but she had reached the age when exploring new territory and having new experiences were often a struggle, especially without her husband by her side. When you live in metropolitan London and everything the city has to offer is a quick bus ride away, you could feel displaced in my "small town in the middle of nowhere" environment, and she did. As she gazed out from the windows of the house one of her early comments was, "Where are all the people? All I see are heads in cars, nobody walks anywhere or stops to chat or wave." In other words, what a strange place my daughter is living in!

I then realized that much of her discomfort was probably due to the same problem I had experienced, the anxiety disorder agoraphobia in which there are repeated attacks of intense fear often related to being separated from your own area of comfort. Here she was three thousand miles from home in what was to her a strange new and hostile environment. Sadly, even her teenage grandchildren were like strangers to her, not having seen them for nearly ten years. I was sure my mother had all the symptoms. I decided to bring her back to something she knew but hadn't been part of for decades. Her music! I gently encouraged and nudged her toward the piano, regardless of her protests. It took weeks before I heard her place her fingers on the keys, and at first, I wasn't sure she could do it. Lavishing praise and more encouragement, sincerely believing that she would soon remember something she had played from years ago, she settled into a quiet daily routine of warming up exercises, which improved amazingly quickly as her fingers became more supple and her confidence returned. I remembered the music she was trying to put together from memory, as a small girl I used to dance around the room as she played the piece. Once a very accomplished pianist, I was soon gratified to hear her reviving something from the large storehouse of music she once knew. Before she returned to England we would have a party for her and by now my mother had become again the lovely lady I knew. She couldn't wait to give a performance for us, and we all danced to the music she played until we were giddy—as she stole the show with a confident and dazzling performance of Edward Grieg's "In the Hall of the Mountain King" from his *Peer Gynt Suite*.

But that was then. Now the year had moved on and it was September 14, 1978, Richard's fortieth birthday when I received the call from my sister in London. Fretting and anxious and fighting back the tears, she gave me devastating news. My mother had been diagnosed with pancreatic cancer. It was advanced and I should return home as soon as possible. My sister's life was unusually busy and complicated, and she had been stretched to fit all the demands into her day. She also needed me to step up and I knew exactly where my responsibilities lay and was anxious to fulfill them.

The late-afternoon sun was losing its warmth and brilliance

but I needed to be alone to digest the news I had just received. With my family's understanding, I grabbed a coat and took off toward the local public golf course. The light was fading gradually, the place was empty, and I needed to walk. I wept and wept with uncontrollable sobs and tears. First my father, then my cousin, and now my mother, all of my dear loves so far away, all gone in such a short space of time. I sat on the top of a rise on an old bench overlooking the peaceful, grassy view the light dropping quickly as the sun began to fade. I was suddenly aware of something, a presence, coming up behind me, but I continued to sit, unafraid, where I was. Within a few minutes I was surrounded by four enormous black dogs, all silently nudging me, leaning against me with their moist noses shining in the twilight. The whisper of a voice behind me reassured me not to be afraid; I was not afraid.

My four fury guardians didn't move from my side; they were known for their giant size, a tremendous strength, their calm disposition, and loyalty. Their thick double coat, muscular build, and strangely webbed feet giving them innate swimming abilities made them an essential choice in life saving in the waters of their home in Newfoundland, Canada. They were Newfoundland Water Dogs. I was grateful for the gentleness and the reassuring peace they gave me and accepted without hesitation the invitation to walk for a while with them and their owner while explaining the anguish and sadness I was carrying. His face still hidden, his voice remained even, soft, comforting, and sympathetic and his four great dogs closely flanked my steps the entire time, one walking in front, one on each side brushing against my legs, one bringing up the rear. They escorted me back to the leafy hole in the hedge where I had eased through onto the course, and feeling again a little like Alice, I went through the space back into the real world with its honking cars and streetlights, the usual noise and movement. In writing about this event over thirty years later its extraordinary details and the effect it had on me remain firmly in an immoveable place in my heart and mind.

I flew immediately home and to the hospital in London and decided as soon as I had been briefed and saw and understood the gravity of my mother's condition that the best thing to do for her was to remove her from the dreary room and uncomfortable bed and the gruff but probably well- meaning staff "sister" in charge and bring her back to her own home where I could nurse her day and night, taking care of all details of her care, and most importantly give her the comfort she needed and my love.

I had always been proud of Britain's National Health System, which for the war-torn British people came with a sigh of relief and brought an amazing and wonderful improvement to their lives, especially needed after the more than five years of enduring the horrors of war, a test that they bravely bore. In 1947, two years after the end of the Second World War, and with Churchill's approval, the new Labor prime minister, Clem Atlee, fought determinedly and won and then signed the new National Health Service into law. I became a small part of that system when in 1958 I proudly began my training to become a state registered nurse. I knew the situation my mother was in, and I knew she needed very personal care from me, now, and in her own home. She was, of course, very pleased to have me there, her own personal advocate, in charge of the situation. I pampered her and fussed over her, gently urging her to try to eat the carefully prepared morsels I put together.

One beautiful autumn day full of mellow colors she felt up for a short excursion, so my sister and I took her to sit in her favorite rose garden in the Royal Greenwich Park, which would have been the perfect peaceful setting except that all the roses were fading and dying. But later, we even found something to laugh about. I learned that a new boyfriend was smitten with her and had brought her a pretty broach to wear on her lapel. He called at the house unexpectedly one day to see her, but I had to keep him waiting quite a while at the door as I rummaged through all her clothes trying to find his gift, then rushed to pin it onto her dress before casually welcoming him inside. Of course, it was the first thing he commented on and was overjoyed to see her wearing his gift. My mother and I laughed at the effort it took both of us to appear nonchalant in his presence. Those first few days she tried to remain cheerful, but her thin, jaundiced appearance told the true story, and soon she was too ill to make it out of her bed. I still tried to feed her with liquid nourishment, which she struggled to sip on, but I could tell it was just an effort to please me. Soon even that gave way to long periods where she only slept. I put a small radio in her room on the BBC twenty-four-hour classical music station and she thanked me with a small smile; the music accompanied her to the end. She was on some pain medication, but the doctor solemnly took me aside and explained that "it" would only be a few weeks, perhaps less. I slept close to her and frequently in the night made sure she was comfortable and checked on her breathing, but I remember making sure I also had a bottle of French Saint Emilion wine close by should I need some comfort myself through those difficult nights. My lovely mother, Zena Emily Pettitt-Garside slipped away into that long dark night, peacefully in her sleep, on October 24, 1978, leaving me with much weighty sorrow to carry back to Schenectady.

The snows finally thawed and the roses bloomed sending a sweetness to the air in Schenedtady's Central Park, which helped heal my heavy sadness. Our sail boat was cleaned and made ready to be the first boat launched into the still chilly lake, and shakily my life went on. I discovered the lovely town of Saratoga with its famous horse racing, gracious elegant buildings and restaurants where we sat with friends, nibbled on hor'dourves, and sipped icy summer gins. We then joined the throng of people who made their way to the attractive setting of the Saratoga Performing Arts

Center, the summer home of the Philadelphia Orchestra, not a bad gig, where we listened under the stars to favorite music played by the excellent orchestra and famous soloists. During the season the space was also shared by the New York City Ballet who delighted us with the "best of Balanchine's challenging steps, danced with the thrill of the latest ballet star Baryshnikov, whose amazing and enormous courage brought him leaping from the Bolshoi Ballet in Moscow's gray shadow, to land happily, solidly and permanently on America's hopeful soil in Saratoga, New York, to the applause and welcoming arms of its people." What a thrill and exhilaration it was to watch this extraordinary dancer jump to those giddying heights; he was audacious! I was so captivated that I volunteered to be sure I could attend every rehearsal and watch him work through his routines for the evening performance—and then I returned for the evening performance; I was that besotted.

We were still sailing at the beginning of September and into October, the air chilling early in this northern clime, but nevertheless, Richard insisted that we be the last boat out of the lake, and most times we were. It was worth staying later to watch in awe the splendid display of leaves changing color everywhere you looked. We sailed silently past a live panorama, and with the ever-changing light, it became a gaudy display, a show of russets, gold, vivid yellow, bright vermillion, scarlet red, and shades of purple. Words were hardly needed.

By this time I was singing again, this time with the Schenectady Choral Society, a local group that had been around for many years. I was drawn by a particular piece they were performing, a favorite of the choral repertoire, the lovely Ein Deutsches Requiem, the German Requiem by Johannes Brahms, composed upon the death of his mother in 1865. Anyone who has heard this piece holds it close to their heart for the beautiful singing and lovely comforting passages. I knew this piece and realized it might

THE RELUCTANT IMMIGRANT

be emotionally difficult to sing in the state of sorrow I was still experiencing, but I wanted to perform it anyway, if for no other reason than to give my own musical tribute to my own mother. It was deeply comforting to me and I gave it my very best, stopping only briefly on a few occasions because my wet eyes made it difficult to read the score. It is difficult not to love this piece and this local group understood and sang with conviction and with sensitivity during its more emotional passages, as in "how lovely are thy dwellings." I liked this group. They loved to sing and I joined them as a full-time member. Overall they did a very decent job and although they were less exciting than the younger Rutgers University group they were nevertheless enthusiastic, and they aimed high. They were directed by a laid-back, middle-aged gentleman who seemed surprised and delighted that so many people turned up every week and wanted to sing and that they were happy to let him direct them. The vocal parts were not very balanced, more altos than sopranos, more basses than tenors. Many of them could read music and the others had a good ear, but more importantly everyone was energetic and very enthusiastic. I was happily welcomed and embraced into the soprano section and then surprisingly introduced to a piece of choral music that I did not know and was not expecting. The standard repertoire was in place and had over the years been done to death but out of the blue came this beauty, which I had never even heard before, and I became quietly overwhelmed and moved in another worldly way the deeper we delved into the score and began to sing and learn the music. The piece was the Rachmaninoff Vespers. Also known as the All Night Vigil. This a Capella gem, which was only for voices with no instrumental accompaniment, was composed as a collection of choral chants by Sergei Rachmaninoff in 1915 during the First World War when traditional Russia was on the brink of destruction and revolution. The composer took the words from the Russian Orthodox Church's All Night Vigil ceremony, which was traditionally sung before religious feasts. "After the 1917 revolution the Soviet government heavily suppressed the church and banned outright all performances of the Rachmaninoff Vespers and they were not heard again in Russia for seventy years!" The Vespers are deeply spiritual but challenging to sing. The language is ancient Russian and it is scored for multiple parts, but the rewards are achingly beautiful and literally life altering for the singers. Nine of the fifteen Vespers use ancient Russian religious chants, some over a thousand years old but the harmonies are exquisitely draped around the chant melodies, and they create a wonderfully rich depth of subtle feelings.

On only one other occasion, many years later, did I have the opportunity to sing this beautiful, but still rarely performed great piece of music. At the end of the Schenectady performance I felt a sense of gratitude, respect, and admiration toward our rather rumpled but always cheerful conductor who struggled with this challenging piece, as we all did. The singing of the Vespers is in itself a form of reward, but at the end of a performance you always know when you have touched an audience, there is a silent pause before the applause begins, and then it seems for a moment that people are reluctant to break their trance and the applause is tentative at first before its volume and enthusiasm comes roaring across the space toward you like a great wave of emotion and of thanks.

My thirst for music and performance opened another door into the Unitarian Church of Schenectady. At a GE social event I met a musical man who loved small, delicate musical pieces written for groups of eight, two on a part. Amici Cantorum was the name of the group and we rehearsed and performed every Sunday at the Unitarian Church, a circular handsome structure with good acoustics and a receptive, well-healed congregation who sat attentively in comfortable seats around the hall even though, as a group, one got the impression they were not quite sure what they believed in on any given Sunday. However, I had learned soon after I had arrived in the United States that it was frowned upon if you didn't have a purposeful date on Sunday morning, preferably one with the Almighty; otherwise, people were uneasy and perplexed and looked at you slightly suspiciously. The Unitarian congregation appreciated our talent and enjoyed listening to our small group of eight in four-part harmony and the lovely early period music we sang, which we performed in between the encouraging sermon and a warm chatty coffee and cookie break. Our dedicated director, one of the PhDs from the research center as his day job, loved this little group and the lovely sound we made together and every week we sang a new, very old piece, to uplift and delight the assembled company.

Outside the signs came early as another winter bore down on us and we were encouraged to do what most of Schenectady's population did, stop fighting the inevitable and join it by taking part in as many of the outdoor activities as possible. The only sport I favored was skiing mostly because of the great gear and flashy winter fashions I could wear. Cross-country skiing was popular with health enthusiasts and we took advantage of being able to walk to the local public golf course, our skis nonchalantly over our shoulders, and rev up our heart rates with the great effort it took to ski half a mile, yes it was a pretty white wonderland, but very hard work for my lungs, but for Richard and the children, it seemed effortless. Both children, however, now in their early teens, hungered for the thrill of the high spectacular mountains less than an hour away by car. It was beautiful and exciting and the lessons were worth it, but jumping off the lift at the top always made me uneasy, wondering if I could control my skis in time before I found myself hurtling uncontrollably down the mountain side followed in hot pursuit by impatient "hot dog" skiers who wanted me out of the way. Richard was also uncomfortable with the speed of the sport from the beginning, and was even more tentative at the top of the mountain than I was. Of course, he couldn't fake it because he didn't even look the part, getting no thrill out of any fashionable winter sports gear! We played the part bravely but our immensely talented children were embarrassed by our puny efforts and tried to avoid being in any way related to us. Mostly we looked forward to an area where we really excelled, the après ski events and there we relished sauntering around in our gear with action-flushed faces playing the part, and where nobody could tell us apart from the real "hot dog" types, unless we were overheard while sharing our fear and dismal performance with each other, so we had to make sure to keep our mouths full of actual hot dogs and those delicious drinks that warmed "the cockles of our heart" as my dad would have said. But then my father wouldn't have been caught dead at the top of a mountain, his "heart and cockles" belonged in the rain and wet mud, blood, and sweat of the rugby field and Richard shared the same sentiment.

The mountains beckoned us on another occasion in February of 1980 when from February 12 to the 24, one of the most superior athletic events of all time was in the making and we were there, almost. The most planned, advertised, and talked about event scheduled to take place at Lake Placid in upper New York State was more like a happening than an event and the eyes of the whole world were watching. We were as caught up in the frenzy and grabbed by the excitement as anyone anywhere and it was taking place within a two-hour car drive from Schenectady. We had to go, and without event tickets we arrived the day before the games began. The games of the 1980 Winter Olympics! Known for its idyllic facilities for winter sports the town of Lake Placid is an extremely beautiful place, on the edge of a pristine arctic blue lake surrounded by high mountains. The compelling town whose population had had an enormous infusion of visitors and international participants shone, sparkled, and glistened in the thin, icy white air. Athletes and their entourage sauntered along with their hot drinks (this is long before Starbucks) mingling with the visitors and all strutted in competition around the town preening in their competitive mode for the best and brightest, the fearless, the fastest, and the strongest all arrayed in the most colorful gear. But the real competition was far more thrilling.

On February 11 we lined up for tickets to the preliminary warm-up ice hockey practice match between the United States and the Soviet Union, who were being touted to win. The Soviet team looked strong and formidable, committed and determined to squash this ad-hoc very young, immature American team. They seemed unevenly matched, the maturity and power of the Soviets dominating almost every move and the atmosphere among the mostly American spectators at the rink was nervous, doubting, worried that from the outcome of this warm-up game the Soviets would smash the US team into the ice and demolish them. Back home on February 22, the date of the actual big hockey game, we huddled excitedly around our television set, hoping that the score wouldn't be too humiliating for the Americans, but what we saw unfold in front of us was unbelievable, a mental and physical transformation had taken place. Gone were the wimpy American college kids about to be thrown to the wolves, deserving of defeat. In their place the team had miraculously grown into their Olympic role. They were strong, disciplined, and organized and in their game plan. They began to run rings around the Soviet Union who didn't know what had hit them. The whole country was in a frenzy of joy over this victory, which was a true David–and-Goliath triumph and became to be known forever as the "Miracle on Ice," and I cheered as loudly as any American on that day for "our" team to win!

Inevitably, corporate shuffles and changes were happening at the labs but Richard continued to enjoy his time at General Electric's Research and Development department. He met and exchanged important new scientific ideas with the brightest and the best from around the world, making many friends among them. His own career really took off, becoming a researcher with new ideas while showing exceptional leadership skills he began to know his own worth, and by the end of the third year, he was becoming well known and admired for some major contributions and a volume of publications of scientific papers. These activities began to be noticed in other companies beyond Schenectady. New job offers began to come his way.

One particular job was very promising. It offered him a directorship with the accompanying rewards and it would mean a move back to a big city on the East Coast. That city would be Boston. I felt as if I was receiving a reprieve, and that this would be my reward for having endured a challenging and difficult four years. He accepted the job at GTE and we were both thrilled and excited and could hardly wait to be Boston bound. Our white house in the woods sold quickly, and as we sped east toward the sea, we looked back, with reassurance, knowing that in spite of the difficulties, the very special friendships we had made in Schenectady, New York, would last a lifetime.

CHAPTER FOUR

Beautiful Boston and the BSO

It was the summer of 1980, and invigorated by the prospect of moving to Massachusetts, I packed up our small house in Niskayuna, New York, with light-footed speed, wearing a permanent smile on my lips. The moving company had been organized and arrived to collect the furniture and the rest of our belongings and to put it into storage until we had found a place to live in Boston, so we were free to leave within a short period of time, but only after attending many memorable farewell parties. All of the new friends we were leaving behind in Schenectady openly expressed their envy at having been offered such a great job and in such a longed for location, and we were assured of receiving many visitors in the months and years to come.

 The journey east would take about three to four hours, driving in new territory that surprised and excited all of us. Leaving New York State behind, we entered a region that I would later come to know well—the Berkshires! The beautiful Berkshires in the western part of Massachusetts reach one thousand feet at their highest point and are punctuated by hills and peaks, rivers and valleys, and in places you could see the sharp buff faces and deep cut gorges through which wide rivers used to run. The area was first discovered during the deadly winter of 1775–76 by Boston-born Henry Knox, one of George Washington's visionary and most valuable generals who seemed to be everywhere during the revolution, from the Boston Massacre to the British surrender at Yorktown. But he is best known for his heroic winter trek to Boston with his artillery. He brought his army with captured cannons, from battles in a place we were already familiar with, that beautiful but deadly spot, Ticonderoga in upstate New York. After crossing Henry Hudson's river, Knox marched 150 miles east with his men, who were known as the "Nobel Train of Artillery" after their travails in Ticonderoga, and they continued on through the Berkshires until they finally arrived in the young city of Boston.

When we arrived in Boston, Richard's new company GTE had arranged for us to stay in a Marriot hotel, which for us, in those days, was a great luxury—it even had a swimming pool, which gave joy to both Beth and Andrew who were feeling the natural uncertainty, anxiety, and insecurity that comes from being uprooted again, which also included the prospect of finding new friends and another new school to get used too. There were justifiable fears, inevitable with all change, usually the experience makes you stronger, but there are those ever-present insecurities that can catch you by surprise and linger long into the future. But companies don't waste time, and as soon as you have signed all the new employment documents, you officially belong to them and must begin to impress immediately, and Richard was happy, willing, and eager to make his mark. The company was good enough to set me up with a real estate lady who knew the area and who could show me an assortment of houses in different places and help to find something that matched with most of the absolute requirements I had about schools and other essentials. I spent some pleasant days being driven around so I could familiarize myself with the wider region and then focused in on one particular house, in one particular area. I wanted to have time to get settled in the house and neighborhood and be sure I could get the children into the best school district in an unpressured fashion, so I didn't dally away my time on the decision making, and after a thorough search, we ended up settling on the first house I had originally seen.

The house was large and handsome, a custom-made, four-bedroom classic brick colonial style, built for its first owner in 1920. It still boasted its beautiful original details of the period, hard wood floors and terra cotta tiles, and it sat comfortably on a generous city-sized corner lot with trees and shrubs and a large screened porch, which quite soon afterward was referred to affectionately by friends and family alike as the party porch. Its front entrance was warm and welcoming with steps leading from the path, to an entranceway with white columns, and at the top of the steps two front doors, one opening first into a vestibule and the second into a wide welcoming hallway with an instant view of the elegant staircase. There were lots of windows everywhere, and in the living room was an impressive and enormous working fireplace with an original and beautiful wooden mantelpiece.

There were so many lovely and unusual add-ons and adornments everywhere. It was my dream house and I immediately loved it. It would also be the only house on the street with a lighted Christmas tree on December 25. But there's more! To my relief it was only a ten-minute walk to the schools and about a fifteen-minute drive into Boston. We had bought a house situated in the attractive city suburb called Newton Center, a desirable, convenient small town with a park and shops and, which, joy of joys, it also had a train station with regular service to beautiful Boston. I was, at last, back in civilization!

The draw of the city of Boston was like a magnet to us, and once we had moved in, we couldn't wait to explore its many pleasures, but first we had to join a yacht club and have our sailboat *Meantime* lowered into the waters of Boston harbor, the Atlantic Ocean. Situated just south of the city of Boston and known affectionately as Southie, it was a funky area offering an array of yacht clubs, bars, and seafood restaurants ranging in price from high end to downright cheap. In the famous Jimbo's Shanty Shack, you could feast on a large delicious lobster for about $8 where in the more up market and fancy restaurants like Anthony's Pier One, a lobster meal would cost four times as much.

At first we enjoyed the fanciful pleasure of buzzing downtown for an evening sail after work, letting the ocean breezes mess up our hair, while tasting the salt left on our lips making us thirsty for a quick beer before the drive home and bed. But we did not extend our yacht club membership a second year and sold *Meantime* for what we had paid for it five years earlier. Perhaps we were just wimpy sailors, but sailing in Boston harbor was a challenge for us, having been used to the placid and picturesque Lake George where the only large vessel that ever came close to posing a threat was the pleasure paddle steamer, the *MinniHaHa*. The harbor in contrast was full of very large shipping, container ships arriving and leaving and generally maneuvering. We were dwarfed by these vessels and we also felt frequently dive bombed by aircraft as we were on the path of the constantly arriving and departing Boston airport traffic. An exciting experience for a while but we hadn't even begun to scratch the surface of this city and we were anxious to do so. It was a cornucopia of delights, with an ever overlapping store of adventures.

To begin with we explored the city together as a family, and Beth and Andrew responded enthusiastically to everything they saw, from the cheerful buzz of Quincy Market, positioned so close to the water you could smell and taste the salty spray in the air on a breezy day. It was actually built in the 1820s on land made by filling part of the harbor. Quincy Market, with its close proximity to the ocean, created a noisy, fun inside and outside atmosphere offering an abundant array of tempting sweets and savories along with live music to bounce along to while munching, or tap to while sitting and casually relaxing at an outside table, just watching the colorful world walk by. A short stroll inland toward the city soon brought you toward the prominent architectural landmarks pointed out on the Freedom Trail. The Freedom Trail was organized in 1951 by an enthusiastic group of local citizens and winds around the city pointing out all the famous tourist highlights, most of which were of great notable national and historical importance. Unlike most American cities, which are built on a grid system, the city of Boston is full of unexpected twist and turns, even cobblestones making it feel more like an old European city, and as you walk through the downtown area, not only do you see an assortment of architectural styles, but among the winding cobbled streets and surprising odd angles, there are many of the handsome, original eighteenth century buildings that are architectural gems and which are still in use today. They have survived because they were originally well built, but also because they have been lovingly cared for over the last two and a half centuries. Like other visiting Europeans we had an instant affection for the place and felt immediately at home in the lovely city of Boston.

As newcomers to the city we were encouraged to get a feel for its important history by walking the Freedom Trail. It is a long trail but the original organizers did help to make it easier for visitors either on a short or long stay to the area to see all the important places and buildings in an organized way. Welcoming, colonially clad volunteers answered questions at various meeting spots, gave directions and a supply of maps, along with abbreviated histories, which the tourists loved. But we were not visitors or tourists. We lived in Boston now and could take our own pleasurable time to peel back and discover the city's history. Having said that, we were as eager as the throngs of day trippers to discover places like Faneuil Hall, which was built in the 1760s on land originally donated to the city of Boston by the French Huguenot merchant Peter Faneuil. This beautiful, iconic market building and meeting house was also the site of many public meetings during the American Revolution. It was expanded in the nineteenth century under the careful eye of the brilliant and famous Boston architect Charles Bulfinch. Mr. Bulfinch was responsible for the numerous plans for grand buildings to be erected on his authority throughout the city and which stand to this day. He set a high standard by choosing the distinctive and notable, redbrick material for most of these handsome buildings, which included the lovely area known as the Beacon Hill Historic District, home over the centuries to many prominent men in national politics, business, and academia.

The oldest surviving house in the city still sits on its original foundation. It was built in what is now known as the North End in 1680, close to Old North church, and it belonged to the revolutionary hero Paul Revere. Perhaps because of its close proximity to the water with a convenient dropping off point for boat loads of people, the area has traditionally been a destination for generations of immigrants. It is still mostly full of the tenement buildings of the period, which housed those immigrants and is now also a lively magnet for artists and well known for its great selection of eclectic restaurants, many of them Italian, and it is affectionately known as the Italian North End. However, in the 1790s, Paul Revere himself was given a role he is not generally known for. He participated in the building of another design by Charles Bullfinch, the Massachusetts State House, built and positioned to impress, which it certainly does, standing at the top of Beacon Hill with a commanding view over the nation's oldest park, the rambling Boston Common. The dome was originally sheathed with copper, which was rolled by the notable local Paul Revere, but during the major additions executed in the 1890s by Charles Brigham, the copper was removed and the dome was recovered with gold leaf. The city was clearly acquiring more prestige along with its wealth and now had gold in its coffers!

The National Historical Landmarks in Boston boasts sixty-one of them on its list so it is possible to walk around the city and its surrounds and always be bumping into something interesting. In cities like London one becomes used to walking with ghosts alongside an ancient history, which goes back more than fifteen hundred years, a history that is constantly being revealed. It is commonplace to find excavators at work all over London at any given time because the remains of those ancient artifacts are still buried a few feet beneath our own feet, just waiting to show us their ancient treasure. We know that the history goes back two thousand years so there are still many stories of the ancient Romans to be revealed, and they wait patiently for us to excavate and discover their world, allowing them to speak to us of their lives stretching back two millennium. Many tantalizing tidbits are revealed frequently from that deep, dark long past period so we keep digging as they spur us on to that end.

England is a secular country now, but the English still love old churches, regardless of the huge drop off in attendance and indeed actual belief over the last century. Both in the country or city, churches are loved. They are loved mostly these days, for their beautiful and inspiring architecture, and again, so many of these incredible buildings with their soaring spires are over one thousand years old. But they are also popular as concert venues because of their great acoustics and generally pleasing atmosphere. It is with awe and reverence that our mouths drop with wonder and our eyes gaze with amazement at the glittering cross gracing the top of a cathedral spire. How did they do it, those daring and dedicated, brilliant master craftsmen, draftsmen, and engineers? Certainly they needed great audacity to accomplish these masterpieces along with their own deep personal belief and faith in what seemed then to be a daunting endeavor, and we love them for their courage and sacrifice and shining success.

Where did Boston get its name, and why is it important what's in a name? As it turns out there is a lot in a name, and this important place name had its origins one thousand years ago. Of course, it harks from the old country, and it was quite usual for the men who became the leaders of a community of immigrants to name their new settlement after the town in the old country from where they had left. About one hundred miles north east of London close to the North Atlantic Ocean lies one of the many "shires" that can be found all over England. A "shire" is the original term dating back to the Norman Conquest in 1066 when the land was parceled up and sectioned off for political convenience, agriculture, and general management.

Boston in Lincolnshire, England, was where the first governor of the new colony came from, his name was John Winthrop. One thought, however, is that Boston's name may also have derived from a seventh-century preacher who originally hailed from France and travelled to the area in England known as East Anglia where he founded a monastery. Saint Botolph was his name, a name with a story that over the centuries took many twists and turns in both place name, pronunciation, and spelling—Botolphston or Botolph's town finally contracted to emerge as the name we know today—Boston. Some variations of this make the old monastery into a small wooden church around 1086 where it is recorded in the Doomesday Book. If you ever take the Freedom Trail tour, you can flounce this tidbit of information and receive an A+ from the guide and fellow trail seekers for a piece of unusual "off the trail" information.

In the city of Boston one cannot help but be drawn to the elegance and grace of all of the old buildings but for me there are four beautiful, notable buildings that deserve special highlighting. Probably the most beautiful is Old North Church sitting not far from the bustle of the Italian North End. It was built in 1723 and inspired by the great English architect of the period, Christopher Wren, whose influence and exquisite style abundantly adorns London's capitol in every direction you may look. In London there is a Wren building on almost every corner of the city, so I'm happy for Boston that it was Wren's whose influence was responsible for the design of Old North Church. It is the oldest church in Boston, and if you have a sense of irony, it was also where Paul Revere ordered lanterns hung "one if by sea, two if by land"—to notify others of British troop movements prior to the Battles of Lexington and Concord.

Old South Meeting House on Washington Street in downtown Crossing is claimed to be the second oldest establishment existing in the United States and is still an active church as well as a museum. It was in this circa 1729 Puritan house of worship that a historic meeting took place. A mass protest, which numbered five thousand colonists, gathered at the Meeting House, which was also the largest building in Boston at the time, to plot and organize the plan that led to the December 16, 1773, rebellion, known as the Boston Tea Party. Since those successful mass protests that led to the Boston Tea Party, the Meeting House continued to serve as a popular gathering place for open discussion and a haven for the celebration of free speech. It was perhaps aptly named and known as the "mouth-house" and became a popular spot for the planning and executing of other revolutionary plots against the British. Clearly a determined congregation, it was where one might look at that feverish time for ongoing plans of rebellion. It was a hot bed of revolutionary resistance and incipient rebellion leading to what ended up as being a successful insurrection.

The third most popular church, I think, is located on Copley Square in an area called Back Bay and was first established in 1670. Old South Church has had many locations during its history, and armed with an ever faithful congregation who picked up and moved on religiously, you could say, to wherever the latest assembly was set down, they finally found their permanent place of worship as we know it today, a building that was built to designs by Cummings and Sears and is now home to one of the city's oldest congregations. Designed from 1870 and finished in 1873, its Venetian Gothic architectural style reflects the new ideas of the time. The style follows the ideas of the British cultural theorist and architectural critic John Ruskin and Old South Church standing handsomely on the corner of Boylston Street and Copley Square, remains one of the most significant examples of Ruskin's influence on American architecture. The old Massachusetts State House was not a church but was home to the state government until 1793 and whose representatives obviously reflected the popular sentiment of the day and continued to place more of the irritant grit into the eye of the British oppressors. It was outside this state house on March 5, 1770, that the Boston Massacre took place. The British clearly had their hands full in this city and the message was "writ large" upon every wall.

In those early months sightseeing and finding our way around in the different sections of the city absorbed us and travelling there by train was a rediscovered delight. I wanted to give both Andrew and Beth more freedom and flexibility and began to encourage them to take the train together at weekends and find their own way around without relying on me to be their chauffeur. I also hoped that by giving them a new status as independent travelers they would enjoy the delights of city life and develop their own city smarts in the process. They had both been born in a great city, and had we still been living London, it would have already been part of their daily existence to travel on busses and trains. It was the easiest and least expensive way to get around. More importantly it made them self- reliant and gave them a sense of responsibility.

When I consider how much ground I covered at the very young age of nine or ten—using my legs, the busses and trains, and later even the underground, being savvy, always making decisions, being in public places, getting yourself to a destination at the right time without being late, either for an appointment, school, or meeting a friend, the sense of confidence in oneself grows and you inevitably become more independent. With the lack of decent, reliable public transportation the need to own one or two cars was normal in the United States, and to my amazement there was sometimes pressure to buy a third car for the use of a sixteen-year-old to get around, which seemed utterly ludicrous to me, and also dangerous. More dangerous for multiple reasons than any problem you could run into travelling on public transport in England at that age. Beth and Andrew appreciated my trust and clearly grew in self-esteem when I announced to them that they had our permission to travel together by themselves into the city at weekends and holidays, watching out for each other at all times, the proviso being that all homework had been properly taken care of before they left. They also had to walk home from the station; this was before the age when cell phones had become attached to every ear. They enjoyed their new status as independent city travelers, and I find it no coincidence that both my children, have never considered living anywhere except in the city, not in the suburbs, which are boring to them, and Andrew, after all these decades has never ever found the need to own a car. I'm proud of them both. Changes and improvements have been made and public transportation is more available in the United States now, mostly in the larger cities, but when compared to the coordinated, modern public transportation systems that exist in all the other cities of the "first" world, it is still difficult to call the American model of public transportation anything but dismal.

By this time a functioning routine was in place. The school transition seemed to be working well and new friends were being made. I was relieved that the academic record of the Newton school district seemed accurate, and based on what I had been told, judging from the curriculum and seriousness of the homework assignments and the generally high expectations of the staff, also the atmosphere and behavior of the students and comments and commitment from teachers. Richard was enjoying his stimulating new job and, of course, needed to let off steam at weekends and again he joined a rugby club, this time a club that boasted to be the oldest and the most esteemed, and some might say most formidable club in the country. The Boston Rugby Club. He was also invited to join the British Officers Club, not because he was or had ever been an officer in the services, but because he was a true Brit with young blood who liked to tell funny stories that helped the whole group to laugh and let off the rest of their steam. The BOC (Boston Officers Club) were very different but also a congenial bunch of mostly "older boys" who had lived and worked in other various colonies and now found themselves, with relief, in the best of cities, Boston. They all loved to get together with their chums from across various continents and ponds and spin out the old yarns from long ago in a harmonious, well-mannered way, while propping themselves up on a "clubby" bar in a respectable part of the city. In slight contrast and not to be confused with, the Boston Rugby Club were also a congenial bunch of mostly younger boys who let their hair down after a bruising encounter with the competing team. Regardless of the winning team, they all loved and respected the rough game that they played and enjoyed celebrating. Only occasionally did the game also include an afternoon of gentle shin kicking but it was all part of the fun. These young men were strong and their teams had remarkable prowess and powers of recovery, and while still covered in the mud of battle, they also clubbed together to quench their thirst, but for this bunch it was in a grubby, unsuspecting bar in a run-down part of town.

With this new move I was feeling a greater sense of inward calm. The anguish and confusion I had carried with me since 1968 was dissipating and I was able to see that my life, indeed the family's life, felt more settled. The weight of grief I had been carrying since the passing of my dearest brother, Danny, and both beloved parents in the space of two years was also less raw, and I was taking stock of where I was and who I was and what positive experiences could be ahead of me. Politics had always been interesting to me for the simple reason that the population of any country stood to gain or suffer profoundly depending on the policies of the elected party.

There was some overlap in ideas between the Labor Party in England and the Democrats, contrastingly, the same between the Tory Conservative Party and the Republicans. I had always stood beside the party that tried to improve the lives of the middle and poorer citizens who needed advocates to speak on their behalf because they had no influence at any level; they were the silent majority. But in America money always has had a penetrating voice and the ballot box was often stuffed with influence from the side of the very wealthy. There were so many improvements that demanded to be made in America as I saw it, especially in areas of education and health care and the environment. The wealthy will always balk at the cost of investing in these basic needs because they can see no personal and immediate profit gain in such an enterprise. This is short-sighted thinking. For real, bold improvement in education and health care both should be seen as an investment in all the people, and in the future of the country. For allowing them to become strengthened and empowered by the freedom that comes from a good education and good health care, it inevitably enables them to better contribute, not only to their own well- being and personal satisfaction, but also to the benefit of the greater and wider society. If those ideas give me a label then I will happily wear it and speak up against the opposing view every time. But I was not an American citizen–yet! I also knew I did not want to be continually standing on the sidelines while I was holding these passionate views. I wanted to be counted, and I needed to vote.

After giving the matter much thought, because it is a huge decision, I decided to apply for US citizenship, which is the first obvious requirement you need if you want to have your views heard at the ballot box. Finally finding myself in a city that I could honestly call home and feeling proud of this city in so many ways, it seemed appropriate to begin the process of applying for my citizenship papers. I will admit that the knowledge that I could also keep my UK citizenship and therefore my passport, making me a dual citizen, made it even more appealing. This sounds like some slightly shady deal, but it was, in fact, a completely legal arrangement that goes back a long way and is also extended to Canadian citizens, though few of them take it up, but I was not going to argue with such a splendid arrangement that became in many ways the final deciding point for me, the icing on the cake. And, of course, from a purely practical point of view, with two passports, the whole thing works wonderfully well when travelling in Europe. When arriving at Heathrow, I can sail through the UK queue (line) instead of waiting at the back of the long, shuffling, and politely grumbling US line (queue). I literally had the best of both worlds, except when that world shifted slightly and I had to give back my lovely UK gold-embossed passport to the authorities because of a new arrangement with Europe. Although Britain was not part of the new European monetary union, it did agree that it made sense to have an "open borders" arrangement, thus the need for one inclusive passport. Of course, there was much grumbling over this in Britain, always reluctant to change the old order of things and people were fond of the distinctive gold regal crest, but in exchange we were given a handsome new, red European Union passport, which replaced it. It expanded the possibilities even more—I could go anywhere.

But I had also reached the point where to have strong opinions about all the pressing issues of the time, was just too frustrating without being able to exercise my right to vote, so I was sincere in my wish to participate at the ballot box; the country needed me! I became a United States citizen on the eleventh of June 1981. The ceremony was held in the beautiful and historic Faneuil Hall and I stood proudly beside more than eighty new immigrants who were originally from almost as many countries from around the world, making my pledge to the flag, Old Glory! It was a very emotional experience for all involved, from the many young and courageous American couples holding and rocking the youngest and newest citizens in their arms—these little ones were the adopted and orphaned babies from Vietnam, to the oldest man who was a shriveled and shuffling ninety-year-old Italian gentleman who had dreamed of becoming an American citizen before he died.

Because I now had the responsibility of the vote I was more properly paying attention to the world of politics, and it did seem that since the late sixties, which was when we arrived, there had been a serious leadership crises characterized by a widespread and deep lack of confidence among the people for the leaders that the system supplied. I saw the sad and struggling aftermath of the Vietnam War was still visible, and it was worn like a collective mask of anguish on the faces of the people. The healing would go on for decades. President Jimmy (Mr. Peanut) Carter still had another five months in office at the time of my naturalization, and although he was considered a dismal failure with most of the voters, I felt he was much maligned. But probably because of his general unpopularity, my new power at the ballot box was going to be undermined since there was not much chance of electing any of the Democratic choices over the next few elections. However…

Anything was better than what had been the embarrassing, illegal debacle that preceded him. Just as a brief reminder, President Nixon's VP Agnew had been forced to resign to avoid criminal charges for bribery. Then the whole gory plot exploded and I thought became positively Shakespearean when Nixon himself was also forced from office for the accumulation of his many sins, which were described in the press as "high crimes and misdemeanors," or multiple serious offences that caught him generally lying and discussing his devious deeds regarding the Watergate cover-up, red-handed on tape! He was removed from office with great drama, being found guilty of a long list of illegal activities, which were related to the fixing of the next election in his favor and included the approval of a break-in and a burglary to obtain information from the Democratic headquarters in the Watergate building in DC. In another era or country, there would have been cries for some serious punishment to be metered out to show an example and dissuade others hoping for high office from undermining the power of the law. But in this era there were persistently loud and angry cries for his resignation and he eventually buckled under their weight and made a dramatic departure.

Allow me to return briefly and wallow a while in the Carter period, because I think it's good to be reminded of where we have been especially if we don't want to go there again. After the Nixon debacle, softly spoken and sincere Jimmy Carter was probably seen as a very clean, very safe slate following the previous mess, especially as his administration sought to make the government more honest and transparent, more "competent and compassionate." But he was often thwarted in his efforts by events beyond his control both at home and abroad. Even though he inherited an economy in a mess, he tried hard and I applauded his positive accomplishments, and by the end of his administration, President Carter had substantively decreased unemployment and had also reduced some of the deficit. He also created the US Department of Education and the Department of Energy and established a National Energy policy. He pursued civil service and social security reform and was the first to see the need to provide a comprehensive health care bill, which I thought was both admirable and essential since all other "civilized" societies had one in place, however, sadly and for the uninsured, the country would have to wait a few more decades to see that come to pass. In foreign affairs President Carter also worked tirelessly for peace in the Middle East, initiating the Camp David Accord, the Panama Canal Treaties and most importantly, the second round of the Strategic Arms Limitation Talks (SALT II). Perhaps he was unpopular because he was honest and straightforward with other politicians including members of his own party, and was "unwilling to pander to the people" he believed to be wrong in their views. He was correct and straightforward on a great many issues, and he practiced what he preached while also introducing many conservation alterations including the installation of solar panels on the White House roof. I thought him ahead of his time–and all of this while keeping an eye on his peanuts!

However, an event occurred far from these shores both in terms of time and distance, which was also far from Carter's influence and ability to resolve. It had begun two decades earlier in the 1950s. I spend time on this because it was as if a heavy cloud hung over the land and as historian Gaddis Smith remarked, "President Carter faced an impossible situation." She went on to remark: "This crises absorbed more concentrated effort by American officials and had more extensive coverage on television and in the press than any other event since World War ll." And it would be this event that would bring about President Carter's demise and become his unfortunate legacy. It was the storming of the American Embassy in Tehran and the forceful kidnapping of sixty-six United States citizens who were held hostage for a period of 444 harrowing days, from November 4, 1979 to January 20, 1981. It seemed to me that the underlying reason for the horrifying debacle was over the vast supplies of oil in Iran and who rightfully owned and had jurisdiction over them.

As a former actor and movie star it was natural for Ronald Reagan to play to the crowd. He had the benefit of a big, genuine smile, good looks, and a charismatic and easy way of communicating with the people. He was immensely popular and well liked regardless of some dubious policies. Although toward the end of his presidency, I and others had the feeling that he had become a puppet on a string and all he had to do was wave and smile and people would shower him with love, but behind the scenes the real work was being done by a staff of frowning faces with suspicious, dull eyes, and I did not approve of many of their conservative policies.

However Ronald Reagan will rightly be remembered for many reasons, first for his admiration, indeed one could even say "love" for the leader of the British Conservative Party, a willfully minded, bombastic woman, admired and also hated alternately by the electorate, but the first female Prime Minister in British history, Margaret Thatcher. President Reagan was decidedly more popular everywhere he went and certainly had more much charm along with a mix of audacity and determination and an American

THE RELUCTANT IMMIGRANT

"can do" attitude for which he was greatly admired across the western world; he also had a winning smile. The Brit and the Yank made strange bedfellows and their personal styles were as different as chalk and cheese, but they both made this audacious challenge to the Soviets to tear down the horrible wall that had separated east and west Germany since the end of WWII. For a while there had been encouraging behind the scenes signs of the possibility of a thaw between the Soviets and the West and Ronald Reagan took full advantage of it, courting a developing relationship with their leader Mikhail Gorbachoff, who had shown signs of warming up the terrible freeze in relationships between the Soviets and the West that had endured since the end of WWII. The nervous situation reached its pinnacle point with Reagan's bold, brave, and some would say improbable demand that would go on to have world shattering consequences and live on in our collective memory for his enormous courage and audacity, but it was past time; somebody who had the courage needed to step forward—it was the president!

In a speech on June 12, 1987, Reagan challenged Mr. Gorbachev in a speech: "General Secretary, if you seek peace, if you seek prosperity for the Soviet Union and Eastern Europe, if you seek liberalization, come here to this gate. Mr. Gorbachev, Mr. Gorbachev, open this gate. Mr. Gorbachev, tear down this wall!" It was a courageous demand and a potentially dangerous challenge at a particularly sensitive time in US and Russian relations. But Reagan stood his own gutsy ground and won, even though it didn't happen until two years later in 1989. The world was ready then and watched in amazement as young Germans from both sides, the east and west of the despised and hated wall that was built to keep them apart, brought out pick axes and hammers and used naked hands and gradually began smashing the Berlin Wall until it started to crumble and collapse into the dust of history. Ronald Reagan was probably the most popular politician in the world, and at that moment in time, and I agreed.

At the next mid-term election the Democrats put up a decent-enough candidate, Walter Mondale, but he was dull compared with the amiable, confident, and always grinning, Reagan. Again, in November 1988 at the end of Reagan's two terms, it was his reliable VP side kick, from a rich dynasty of oil-lucky Texans, George Herbert Walker Bush, who went over the finish line, leaving my guy the Democratic candidate, Dukakis the Greek, literally in the Tank! But G.H.W. Bush only made it for one term– perhaps the country was waking up–and finally they elected a young, charismatic Democrat from the South called William Jefferson (hopes of grandeur) Clinton. A colorful character who would do a great deal of good for the country, and as it happened, for my family personally, while he also found time to entertain and outrage his friends and foes alike, along with the general populace, with his appetite for human antics. It was a love-hate relationship, but more of that later.

American politics were many things—interesting, perplexing, complex, frustrating, and also confusing but I felt compelled to follow them so as to better understand the country where I was now a citizen with a vote. But I had three important items on my own agenda that I was very serious about, and they were as far from politics as they could be. I wanted to sing, start a business, and write, roughly in that order and then juggle them all at the same time, as competently as I could.

Happily Boston had a rich musical life and I had many choices. To get my voice warmed up I joined a local choral society in Newton, and there I met my first friends who were both fun and interesting to be with. They took me under their wing and introduced me to many places and people in the area, and we are still in touch all these decades later. But I wanted more. This first choral group was too easy for me so I soon switched to a more challenging group, which I liked better and where I made even more friends. I enjoyed this group immensely. The music was unusual and challenging and the fine director Dr. Allan Lannom was meticulous in his standards and demands on us. The group had a fine reputation and gave concerts twice a year in Sanders Hall, which was part of Harvard University and across the Charles River in the city of Cambridge. The lovely, gracious concert hall with the original, attractive aged wood paneling and décor, and with generally good acoustics, was one of many old and interesting buildings belonging to the University, and we always performed to a packed house. Many years later, living in a different state, many hundreds of miles from Massachusetts, I was caught off guard while listening to National Public Radio. I heard the host announcer speak a few heartfelt and unexpected words at the end of her program, news that made me gasp with surprise and sadness as it flooded my mind with many happy memories— Allan Lannom, who had many musical friends and followers across the country, the director of the Masterworks Chorale in Boston, had died. The announcement was followed by music recorded by my old chorus and I could feel the sad news reverberate nationally across the radio waves.

In November 1981, a dreadful event occurred that would change the lives of our family for many years, if not decades to come. Beth, was seventeen years old and, for a little extra pocket money, had found herself a job at a bakery in Newton Centre, and it was an easy distance for her to walk to and from home. She was happy with herself, and her scholastic accomplishments, which were many. Her school work had always been excellent, and we knew she would soon be accepted to a university place. She could have applied to any of the colleges in Boston, but she wanted to broaden her search, and she was offered a scholarship to a university in Chicago. However, she wanted to go even farther afield and applied and was accepted to Canada's "Harvard," McGill University in Montreal.

But on that dark November night, it seemed as if all would be lost. She usually finished at her job at 9:00 p.m. and was home shortly afterward. On this particular night she was late. Richard had retired to bed and was already asleep, and Andrew was staying with a friend. I called her place of work but clearly it had closed. No one was there to answer to phone. I waited and waited pacing up and down. I took the car to see if I could find her but came back to the house, afraid to miss her if she had called or perhaps taken a different way home. This was before cell phones and so the instant gratification of a quick reassuring call or message was not possible. Just before eleven o'clock the home phone rang and I raced to catch it on its first ring expecting to hear Beth's clear voice maybe needing a ride or at least with a reason for her lateness. A woman's voice I did not know spoke with an official tone and asked to speak to Mrs. Neville. I told her I was Mrs. Neville. "Do you have a daughter called Beth?" she asked. My legs were beginning to shake as I answered, "Yes, I do." Quite calmly the woman informed me that there had been a car accident and that Beth had been taken to the Newton-Wellesley Hospital. "Can you come as soon as possible? Do you have transport? Do you know the way?" "Yes, yes," I replied. Shaking badly I mumbled some inaudible words and replaced the phone receiver and stood silently in the half light of the room, choking back the sea of sobs I knew I must control.

First I had to wake Richard who had not stirred. I began to shake his shoulder to rouse him not wanting to scream with distress and anxiety. I had to wake him gently or it would be too much of a nightmare shock for him. He gruffly came out of his deep sleep, grumbling and wanting to know why he had been woken up. "It's Beth," I whispered. "Beth has had some kind of car accident and they have taken her to Newton-Wellseley Hospital—they just called, no details, but they want us to go there right away. Get in the shower. It will wake you up," I urged. Still stunned from shock and from being wakened from a deep sleep, he staggered into the shower. "I have no other news, only that we should get there quickly."

We drove in silence along the ill-lit empty roads on that cold and dark November night, our hearts throbbing and our minds racing, not knowing what horror awaited us, all the while just wanting to hold our beautiful daughter in our arms. The ER was swarming with medics, police, and firemen, but we were whisked immediately into a small room off the ER where the head ER doctor was ready to speak to us. It was like living a nightmare. He told us there had been a serious accident involving Beth, the passenger. The driver had missed a curve in the road and had driven head-first at high speed into a group of very large, old trees spread out along the sidewalk. Without a seatbelt, Beth had been thrown forward and was found unconscious in a fetal position under the dash board, which had collapsed over and on top of her, trapping and sealing her in this small metal cage. Unfortunately her head had taken the full impact.

The Jaws of Life had managed to remove her by cutting her out from underneath the car. She had multiple injuries, which he proceeded to list. At this point my reaction was to put my hands over my ears and blot out this dreadful news. I couldn't listen to anymore and I sat shaking and sobbed silently. At first the shock was so immense that you feel as if every drop of blood in your body has been drained away and any attempt to move would result in a complete physical collapse. The doctor couldn't even give us a prognosis because they were dealing with multiple injuries and they still had a long list of tests to do. After a few sips of coffee I regained a strange, almost animal strength and a strong determination to see my daughter immediately. The doctor shook his head–not a good time—but I could not wait another second and insisted, and ignored him, rushing out of the little office across the two steps to where I knew Beth was. With nurses trying to restrain me I pushed through the door marked "No Admittance," into the blinding light of the treatment room. "I just want to see her," I whispered. Surrounded by about a dozen doctors and nurses I peeked through the small spaces between their busy hands. And there she was. My beautiful daughter lying naked on a flat board on the raised top of a hospital bed. She was even more precious to me at that moment than she had ever been. She seemed asleep. Her skin was smooth and white and unblemished. I ignored the sticky, matted state of her hair; to me it still looked glorious. Her long dark wavy hair was still shining, framing her perfect face, which had not even a scratch on it. Renoir would have loved this young woman, for that is what she looked like, a rich, breathtaking Renoir painting.

How could she have so many injuries? I hadn't seen a single one. Perhaps they were all mistaken and she could come home with us this very night. At this point I quietly allowed myself to be escorted from the room, still distraught. I was determined to believe that she would make it. She was alive, and at that moment I had to sustain myself with positive thoughts and the hope that my daughter would survive.

How we made it home is a blur. Like zombies we just sat staring into space, uncomprehending, hardly able to replay in our minds what we had just witnessed and what the doctors had told us. At this stage her medical team was not making any promises—many more tests still had to be done. It would take days, maybe weeks to give us all the answers. Right now she would be under twenty-four–hour surveillance until further notice. Beth was in the deep sleep of a coma, her skull fractured, a concussion and a brain stem injury, and we were only just beginning to learn what all that might mean.

Richard and I blundered as if blinded by shell shock through the next few days. Reading the report of the accident in the paper was surreal. Taking calls from Beth's distressed school friends and teachers then making the mistake of morbidly looking at the wreckage mostly because Andrew and his friends wanted to see it. I think perhaps they needed to gawk at the scene because until they had been confronted with the evidence they couldn't imagine the seriousness of the accident and the evidence solidified its harsh reality. Andrew was very close to his sister and was naturally distraught, and I worried about his on- going emotional reaction especially when a few weeks later he was diagnosed with alopecia, which often occurs after a deep shock. He looked like a sad little monk with a smooth circle of hair missing from the top of his head. The house was nevertheless always full of young people calling at the door for any news about Beth, while also taking Andrew under their wing. It was comforting to know that they had both already made so many friends and that they had all been so touched by the accident. But Richard and I didn't know very many people locally; we were pretty much on our own. I called our old Schenectady friends and they set up a network of calls among the group so that we had lots of people telephoning for news, sending flowers, and giving support. Our close friends Eileen and Himanshu from Schenectady simply dropped everything the moment they heard the news and were at our door, after a three-hour drive, to hold and comfort us. There was a great outpouring of concern, support and encouragement, food and flowers as people began to hear the news. At the hospital Beth was still in a coma and being held in the intensive care unit surrounded by gurgling tubes and flashing monitors, looking just like sleeping beauty waiting for one of us to kiss her awake, so we tried kissing her and talking to her and stroking her hair for what seemed like hours, both of us only being able to imagine the real response that we so desperately longed for. I tried to reassure us by saying that she was still healing and simply wasn't quite ready to give us her smile.

Beth had a wonderful dedicated team of first-class professionals of at least a dozen doctors and nurses who checked on her constantly, watching for any signs of change, updating us all the time about what they were doing. Beth was basically in this state of healing for about a month, but in the third week, we received a call from her neurological and general surgeon who wanted to see us, and with lightning speed we were in his office. Not wanting us to overreact he announced carefully, "I don't think I'm going to have bad news for you. Beth's face has begun to twitch and her eyes have begun to flutter, not absolute but possible signs that she might be slowly coming out of her coma," he said calmly. He cautioned us that while this was normal, it was not necessarily a guarantee of overall improvement. We went from his office into the intensive care room where Beth was being cared for. She looked exactly the same each time we visited—in a deep slumber, my perfectly beautiful daughter. The doctor explained reassuringly that the experiment he was going to perform "might appear to be a little rough on her." He was about to put his physical weight on her sternum by pressing down hard on it. It was meant to be painful, the theory being that on some level she would feel it and that the discomfort would rally her and exact a response. It seemed a strange test and was hard to watch and I remember saying, "You're hurting her. Please don't do that!" He repeated this pressure test several times and I saw a little frown appear across her forehead as if she were trying to understand this puzzling pain. And then we witnessed the result we were all hoping to see. Slowly and miraculously Beth began to open her eyes, just a little. The doctor kept calling her name loudly, almost shouting at her. Then when he thought he had her attention on some level, he asked her a question. I suddenly realized the huge consequences related to this question. If Beth answered it meant that she could hear. If she answered correctly it meant she could understand, and it meant that she had sight and it meant that she could also recognize us. Pointing to me the doctor asked, "Beth, who is this lady?" Followed by, "Beth, who is this man?" The response was slow and almost incoherent but the sound Beth made was a word which I understood as being "Mum," and the second sound was a word, which we understood as being "Dad." Through our tears of joy we were all jubilant with relief and felt enormous hope because in this strange medical test, we knew Beth had reassured everyone that she was definitely going to make it, even though as soon as the doctor removed his weight from her sternum, she fell back into her healing sleep.

The news brought all who knew and loved Beth great joy. But it was still early days and she faced a difficult struggle to regain her hearing, speech, and vision. Now out of intensive care she was in a private room and was allowed limited time visits from family. A sign on the door read, "Please identify yourself. Beth has difficulty with hearing and vision." She was also having difficulty with her speech. We noticed she brought her index finger up to her lips to help move them. Her doctors explained that the injury to the brain stem had left her face with some paralysis, but that with time and therapy most of it would improve although nobody could give us a time frame for this. For our therapy Richard took up jogging at least a mile and aimed at adding extra distance every day, which he did. My therapy was being by her side every day, and even though she was asleep most of the time, I spoke softly in her ear hoping she could hear me. I bought many different products and brushes so that I could gently brush her hair. I had to do this slowly and in stages without giving her any awareness of discomfort. It was so matted with different substances that it took me ten patient days of gentle brushing, strand by strand, before her long beautiful hair took on any resemblance of its former glory. Poor Andrew, who had been very badly affected by this family tragedy, was a gentle, brave, loving son and brother, and he quietly, almost spiritually, accepted the strange but sweet circle of smooth baldness visible in the middle of his thick head of hair and he wore about him a quiet sense of solace, which he eagerly extended to us and to all who came in contact with him. I never received an understandable reason for this strange hair loss, except that Alopecia was caused by extreme stress, which he had certainly, quietly, and stoically experienced as a result of Beth's accident. Although different in many ways, Andrew and Beth had always been very close.

Like a Christmas miracle, Beth was allowed to come home on Christmas Eve. It seemed too early to me. She was very shaky and at first practically immobile, needing a wheelchair, and I worried how she would cope. She had also dislocated her hip and needed a walker to aid in balance and a little later, walking. We had instructions to place alternate patches on her eyes to strengthen her vision in each eye separately, and she continued to use her finger to move her lips to help her form words. Mostly Beth lay on the couch and slept, rallying when a friend arrived to see her. It was also difficult for her friends who were shocked when they saw her and it was very difficult for Beth to have them see her in this compromised position, so unlike her old self. Before this accident had happened, with her sunny disposition and great sense of humor, she was very popular and had a positive effect on everyone she met. Mostly, everybody was stunned, shocked, and saddened. Late one evening before she left the hospital she called me. The reality of her situation was catching up with her – "Mum," she said, "I want to cry but no tears will come because my face is paralyzed." I comforted her and thought but did not say, "Well, my darling girl, I'll weep enough tears for both of us." Which I surely did.

The freezing and depressing Boston winters had to be endured, but they certainly did not help our mood and there was still much that had to be done to help Beth. She continued to make progress slowly and among the many visits to various doctors and specialists and scheduled therapies one of her outings was to the hospital for ear surgery. The fierce impact of the accident had displaced one of the small bones in the middle ear, which had lodged itself out of place on the inside of her cranium and could not be retrieved and so it was replaced with a prosthetic bone, which considerably helped improve her hearing, a very positive result for her.

The Newton school policy was for any student in a similar situation, where poor health or any infirmity prevented a child from physically being in school, to be provided a tutor. Of all the essential physical therapies that Beth was involved in this connection back to the world of school and studies was probably the most important. There were still many difficult challenges but they were not insurmountable. We would not let them be, and with the care, help, and patience shown by us and her tutor along with Beth's own strong determination, our daughter was soon able to see her old dreams returning, and by focusing her mind on positive goals, she could also lessen her own physical insecurities. I began to see her old confidence and strength peeking through, tentatively at first, like the earliest green shoots of spring daffodils daring so courageously to push through the gradually thawing but still hard New England soil.

Life, of course, goes on a pace. In spite of the great trauma and the lengthy aftermath of recovery, Beth managed to do extremely well on her SAT's and advanced placements and was offered a place at McGill University in Montreal. She had several offers but the allure of a different country and French culture was irresistible. But it was very hard leaving her there alone at her new campus home in Queen Victoria Hall as she was still fragile and struggling to accept a new reality, which was difficult. She wanted to make a bold statement about herself, and do something that she couldn't hide from. So being Beth, both brave and strong, she decided to cut all her lovely long dark hair very short and dye it bright red! Even though I shed a few tears at her decision, I so admired and completely understood why she had decided so drastically to change her look. It would have been too easy for her to hide behind her long hair, but she needed to show the world the new Beth, and be damned, she did! What a girl!

I cranked up the heat in our lovely old house and tried to give Andrew more attention and encouragement. He continued to delight and entertain all of us with his piano playing and his good looks and his genuinely warm and affectionate personality made him very popular.

CHAPTER FOUR
PART TWO

If Music Be the Food of Love

After the pain and anguish of Beth's accident, I wanted to regain some balance in my own life, and the only way to do that was to return to music and singing and pursuing my passion as far as it would go. I decided on courses in general music studies, including sight reading and also voice lessons, and I found a wonderful voice coach who had taught at the New England Conservatory of Music. Her name was Fran Kenoff and I thought of her as a musical soul mate because from the very first lesson with her and over the many continuing years of lessons with her, she changed my life. Fran Kenoff worked me hard every week and challenged me in so many ways. Technique, technique, technique was what it came down to. It takes years to train your voice as well as your body so that you can place yourself in a concentrated state of relaxed control every time you have to sing a single note, a place where you are able to quietly command "the voice" to produce the sound you want or need for any piece of music at any given time.

After a while changes in your physique become natural and

permanent. Your back becomes straighter, your shoulders comfortably down and relaxed. You learn to naturally make adjustments as you shift your posture and become more conscious of the way you are breathing. Your diaphragm, a muscle you rarely think about, becomes the most important muscle in your body as it helps control the whole breathing process essential for a good technique, and it takes over your thinking. Then your body gradually eases into a relaxed state of readiness should it be needed to produce the physical and mental state of being for the singing of a single note. I only knew the French language, but Frances worked on teaching and correcting my pronunciation in half a dozen languages, including improving my French. And so we worked every week on the vocal literature and picked pieces to represent at least five hundred years of composition. Passion and physical expression were only allowed within the parameters of the technique, even when lying flat on the floor or in some other unusual position. Agility being an essential requirement for opera singers was also part of my vocal instruction from Fran Kenoff, just in case. Anything less took away from the control and balance of a perfect technique, which is what you strive years for but rarely completely achieve. Fran Kenoff turned me into a soloist. I have countless memories of this period of growth, and when she asked me my ambitions, I replied that I would love to be good enough to sing in the Boston Symphony Orchestra Chorus. Her face broke into a beaming smile, and as if she were throwing down the gauntlet, she said, "What are you waiting for? You belong in that chorus!"

I had practiced and prepared for months for the event that was looming in front of me, the afternoon of my audition with the Boston Symphony Orchestra's chorus master, John Oliver! I had been well prepped by my coach and my fate and musical future depended on remembering everything I'd been taught while also keeping positive and believing that my audition would go well. I checked and rechecked all the important aspects of my technique while trying to keep my nerves steady as I paced up and down outside Symphony Hall, until my watch told me it was time for my appointment and time to literally face the music. John Oliver knew exactly what he was looking for in a voice. Brightness. Clarity. He demanded a "forward" sound that would resonate in the frontal cavities of a singers' face or "the mask"—a sound that almost came through your eyes. He wanted a sound that would never be swallowed or mushy or indistinct, but a sound that would pierce then penetrate through any orchestra, to the back of any concert hall in the world and connect with the ears of the audience in the last row, making them thrill, tingle, and tear with emotion. It was a sound I naturally had, but Fran Kenoff had honed that sound using multiple techniques so that its placement was reliable and exact. The audition took less than half an hour, beginning with a brief interview about studies and experience and then listening first alone to the range and position or placement of the voice followed by sight reading with sheet music to check reading ability alone, followed by singing my voice part together with a SATB quartet. Floating out of the studio on a cloud, I gave a huge sigh of relief. There then followed the inevitable agonizing hours afterward, as I paced up and down, my stomach in knots, as I dealt with a continuing inward assessment of how well I had actually performed during the audition, or not! I had also learned that for the first three years as a chorus member, these auditions were a yearly event keeping every member of the chorus on their vocal toes and in training continuously. If all the requirements had been satisfied during that period you were, safe from auditioning again for a three-year period. The letter arrived within the week, inviting me to become a member of the Boston Symphony Orchestra Chorus, also popularly and affectionately known, far and wide, as the Tanglewood Festival Chorus, where I stayed as a proud, permanent member for nearly ten years.

Among the citizens of Boston there had long been an interest in symphonic music and there must have been much rejoicing when the Boston Symphony Orchestra was handed a beautiful new concert hall in which to celebrate and show off its talents to the full. So it was in 1900, with great fanfare, that the Boston Symphony Orchestra moved into its permanent home, the newly completed Symphony Hall, which later also included the Boston Pops. Symphony Hall is now an official national historic landmark but derives its significance not only from its architectural and acoustical prominence, but also from the influential role the BSO has had in shaping American musical culture for more than a century. It also boasts the finest acoustics of any concert hall in America and is among the top three concert halls in the world for that reason. Constructed in the Italian Renaissance Revival style, the *Boston Herald* commented at the time, "No more brilliant or important event has ever figured in the musical history of Boston. Symphony Hall made an indescribably charming appearance with its flood of electric lights, its chaste and harmonious coloring, the modesty, yet effectiveness of its ornamentation—the

THE RELUCTANT IMMIGRANT

broad aisles and the ease with which visitors could reach and leave their places— met with instant appreciation." I should include here the fact that today's patrons still sit on the original leather seats in the auditorium, and while they offer reasonable comfort, some wriggling can be seen from the stage from time to time, and there can be heard the occasional muffled grumble. Of course, it is what happens on stage inside the hall that really matters and on this score the BSO has consistently retained its high place on the international scene, attracting the greatest conductors and soloists for over a century. There have been eleven conductors mostly from the northern European climes, and a knighted Englishman, a Frenchman, and a Japanese gentleman were among the group. Sir George (Serge) Kouseivitsky held the baton firmly and for the longest duration from 1924 to 1949. And the enduring and popular name of Arthur Fiedler was synonymous with the Boston Pops serving as he did as maestro magnificent from 1930 to 1979.

My tenure with the BSO was just short of that of the Seiji Ozawa reign (1979–2002) and I consider myself deeply privileged to have been able to sing in the chorus under his direction during that time. An inspirational leader, Maestro Ozawa conducted with great intensity, and he succeeded in gradually easing his audience away from the former dominance of the German hierarchy of composers by bringing to the audience many new and rarely performed pieces, some even semi-staged, conducting always from memory, and with a piercing eye-to-eye connection with the chorus that was, at first, a little intimidating, but we were rewarded when he was pleased with us as he beamed his ready grin and always showed his appreciation for our performance graciously.

From Carl Vigeland's book *In Concert* about the life of the BSO and the preparations leading to a famous Mahler concert and subsequent recording of his Second Symphony, John Oliver and the chorus are discussed. "Welcome to the new season," said

John Oliver to the chorus, fully assembled for the first rehearsal for the Mahler 2. Perched as usual on his stool, one foot on the floor and the other on a rung, John held his glasses in his left hand and a baton in his right hand, and in the spirit of congratulation he said, "It's really hard to get into this chorus. That's a great thing! I never get tired of auditions. The whole psychology of them, of the people, is fascinating. Bravo to all of you for your success and continued interest." Though he would not give many more such pep talks, he felt this one was necessary to invigorate his singers, as if we needed it! John Oliver is the one who has to worry about getting everything correct for Seiji Ozawa. And John was under pressure on that first night of rehearsals for the Mahler 2 symphony. He knew that when Seiji met the chorus for the first time, the night before the first orchestral rehearsal, he would expect the same perfection he demanded of his own professional orchestra members. Should the chorus fail to meet those demands in any way, the impact on the performance would be disastrous, and John Oliver might be out of a job.

Supremely confident, John never hesitated in his directions to the chorus. He knew precisely what he (and Seiji) wanted and expected the singers to do exactly what he said. The chorus sings in the symphony's fifth movement, a total of four times, alone and with soloists and orchestra. But the most critical moment is the very first moment, and John spent much of this rehearsal (and I remember subsequent rehearsals) stressing to the singers that they begin their entrance with "barely a murmur"—triple pianissimo as I remember it, an almost inaudible whisper. This is vital to demonstrate the very, very gradual increase in volume and intensity as the music progresses toward its triple forte climax. It must hold back on the increase in volume at the beginning until in the final measures of the piece its fortissimo becomes thunderously loud, expressing overwhelming triumph. As John left Symphony Hall at the end of the auditions for that season, he could see the dark stage as he passed it. His chorus would stand there on opening night, and with the orchestra, and perform Mahler's great second symphony. He remembered back to his graduate days when he'd had a season seat in the second row and had to crane his head to watch Eric Leinsdorf the BSO's conductor between 1962 and 1969. *Music*, he thought, *music lifts us all out of our little lives!*

I thought the idea of memorizing every score, which had become a standard "pride" in the chorus over the years, came originally from Seiji. He obviously had a photographic memory himself and only rarely referred to the score. The chorus bent only gradually under pressure at first because it was such a time-consuming burden, but we did come to terms and acceptance. The theory behind it being that when you have internalized a piece of music, you claim it as your own and can involve yourself in the piece more deeply and expressively, unencumbered by page turning and holding a heavy score. It did, of course, also have the added and required result in having us being hypnotically glued to Maestro Ozawa throughout the entire performance. While theoretically we accepted all the pluses of this approach, at that time when the idea was still relatively new, most chorus members believed there was a vanity element at play, which at first we puzzled over, but memorization of a score had developed into an unavoidable way of life if you wanted to be a full member of a famous orchestral chorus, so the grumbling faded away, and we accepted it as a way of life.

In the early years I remember spending hours every day studying and memorizing Bach's B Minor Mass, no mean feat, in fact a huge undertaking, especially while travelling on a personal pleasure trip to Europe. My score came with me and was always in my hand and so it felt more like a business trip, and some of the time I missed seeing many of the sights! We sometimes grumbled collectively and shared funny stories and even memorization tricks, but we were all passionately committed to the chorus, and to our beloved leader John Oliver, who, often with the help of his dry humor, put us through our paces, honed our collective talent and skills until we shone with warmth of tone and brilliance of clarity, bringing joy like the sun, and winning with wonder the hearts of all who heard us sing! There were even out-of-town trips woven into our busy schedule. Every year we were invited to travel to New York City for the opening concert of the season at Carnegie Hall. It was always such an exciting thrill mostly because the hall itself was such a beautiful place to be; its grace and simple elegance took your breath away. But New York City always accelerates the energy level, and in the short time we were there, we made hay while the sun shone—a quick stroll in Central Park, in and out of a few galleries, window-shopping down the avenue and lunching in favorite restaurants. One of our most popular places was the Russian Tea Room conveniently located a few paces from Carnegie Hall, and after the performance, we were very hungry. Singing gives you a great appetite, and we ordered nearly everything on the menu. We didn't even care when we discovered that most of the handsome, flirting, and perfectly uniformed Cossack waiters working there were not from Moscow or St. Petersburg or even the Russian steppes, but from the Bronx!

The schedule was extremely demanding since on top of the rehearsal and performance demands there were also recordings and the extra personal time for memorization. When one considers, that in addition to those requirements most members of the chorus also had a full-time job, it meant for a very full schedule! I was one of the more fortunate members having at this time started a home business, which gave me more flexibility. The BSO management had in place a concert series of three dates in a given month, which allowed the audience some flexibility as to which evening fitted their personal schedule. Nearly every month the chorus was required to perform a newly prepared work three times over, so in the course of the performance year, we would sing approximately twenty-four concerts. John Williams also directed us during the popular and fun Christmas Pops season in November and December. The Pops, as they were affectionately referred to, were frequently televised, and he produced new pieces yearly for us to perform. Our schedule required that we perform two or three concerts a week under his direction, so add up to another twenty Boston Pops performances to the tally.

In July and August, the orchestra moved to its summer home at Tanglewood in the Berkshires where the chorus was also required to perform maybe three or four pieces during that period either in recital form or with the orchestra. When you add at least one regular rehearsal per week plus the dress rehearsal to prepare the work for performance, it was quite a demanding schedule. However, we learned early on that it was your very own responsibility to apply yourself and work alone on learning the music and text, in other words, sight read the music and then memorize the piece on your own. The coming together in a group rehearsal was not, repeat not, for note learning. It was for the purpose of balance, phrasing, intonation, articulation, emotional expression, and the many other nuances that elevate a performance from the ordinary to the memorable, and even to spectacular, so that the experience for us and for the listening public would hopefully stay in everyone's memory for a lifetime. We were the lucky ones. Successful at our auditions and regardless of the sometimes grueling demands we were happy to commit to a rehearsal and performance schedule of up to seventy dates over the course of the year, which would require most of us to rearrange our whole lives during the peak weeks. And yet, even with such a hectic year-round schedule we never faltered. We laughed heartily, and often, we supported each other tirelessly on and off stage, we wept frequently from emotion, we delivered passionately for each performance, and year after year, we came back for more. Because we knew that the experience was exceptional in all respects, we gave every ounce of our being to it and still we all felt humbled and privileged to be a part of something so memorable, so powerful, beautiful, and life changing in all the best ways. I was strongly aware that in a very real sense I was fully participating in my own life and that in future years, when looking back, I would know that these were indeed the very best years of my life.

In the early summer of 1984 the BSO management received an unusual request from the BBC Symphony Orchestra in London concerning their UK and European Premier of Sir Michael Tippett's new work, *A Mask of Time*. Like his contemporary Benjamin Britten, Michael Tippett had deeply held humanitarian and pacifist views and was a conscientious objector in WWII, and this large, deep, and challenging work reflected all of those sentiments. This much-anticipated and lauded work for orchestra, chorus, and soloists was conducted by Sir Colin Davis and lasted approximately ninety-five minutes. It was given its world premiere by the Boston Symphony Orchestra and the Tanglewood Festival Chorus in Boston on April 5, 1984. I remember well the struggle the chorus had in leaning the difficult piece, which we pulled together and eventually triumphed over after hours of extra work and rehearsals. It was very challenging and we all agreed that it was indeed the most difficult choral piece we had ever had to perform. But we were extremely fortunate in having the great Colin Davis, whose graciousness and patience stayed by our side during the whole process. We were also entertained when Sir Michael Tippett himself arrived to observe one of the later rehearsals clad entirely in a soft white, sublime cloth, looking rather tanned and biblical as he seemed to float in air as the head of a religious processional, an entourage of beautiful, tanned young men also in white drifting silently a few respectful steps behind their esteemed leader, down the aisle toward the stage. I believe, for once, we all took our eyes off the conductor as we observed this eye-popping spectacle!

The great acclaim that followed our premier had reached the world and especially the chorus master of London's BBC chorus who were having difficulty with the demanding and complicated score, even though Sir Michael was one of their very own, and they needed the support and help for their upcoming premier at the summer promenade concert series, and thought of us! Would it be possible, they wondered, for a group of singers from TFC to be kind enough to come to London to swell the ranks of the BBC singers. The Brits needed the Yanks! They would give us accommodation and feed us and give us expenses, but we had to provide our own air fare. Even with that it was an event I had to participate in—I would have been happy to swim to London to be part of the occasion. Generous Richard was on my side and graciously agreed I could take the time and the money and my voice to help out my fellow Londoners in their hour of need, on the great stage where I had sung as a young girl. I was delirious with excitement. I was still in contact with my old music teacher who had taken me to the Royal Albert Hall to sing with the London Schools Choir when I was eleven years old, and I telephoned her immediately with the good news, which gave her time to buy a ticket and be witness to this great event. We were very warmly received when our group arrived a week before the July 23 debut. One felt an almost palpable sigh of relief from our hosts when about twenty-five TFC members arrived in London for our first rehearsal with the BBC chorus. We had been studying this score for months and also had had many extra rehearsals before we felt that we had conquered the massive piece. We had struggled with the beast and made it compliant and then we had ridden the composition successfully into performance and had received the great acclaim we deserved that came from far and wide, so we knew the many snares and pitfalls and how to prepare and how to avoid them. After a few rehearsals, confidence shone shyly on the faces of the brave Brits as they tackled the extreme complications of this great English composer's latest masterpiece, the *Mask of Time*. Smoothness appeared around the rough edges and faces beamed with relief and delight as the combined chorus turned the performance into another triumph for the composer. The UK and European Premier was considered "undoubtedly the most exciting occasion at the BBC Promenade Concert Series for that year." Meeting with my old teacher after the performance she declared how proud she was to see me on that stage again and that she had been "so very impressed, my dear" by the concert even though she quietly confessed, "It was just a little too modern for me, my dear."

Coming down to earth from such giddying heights was difficult and finding a balance usually required finding a quiet place to decompress and internalize before the next performance. Discovering yoga helped enormously.

So did discovering English hand-colored copper restrike engravings! Over the years on my visits back to London I would sometimes break away on my own and revisit some of my favorite "out of the way" haunts to find unusual galleries and bookshops. There are numerous small galleries that show and sell old prints, mostly run-offs, sometimes hand colored, which I had purchased over the years. But I was always asking questions of the gallery owner, trying to find more unusual and more expensive prints with the idea that if I found something interesting I could ship them back to Boston and hopefully sell them. Boston, I thought, would be the perfect market for the right artwork, and they would be a great fit especially when hung in the lovely old eighteenth-century homes in the city, in areas like Beacon Hill. Perseverance finally paid off and I found three very good galleries in London who sold hand-colored restrike engravings from the original copper plates. I bought some and carried them back to Boston, then immediately had them framed and hung them in my own home. They were magnificent, and seeing them on the wall, I knew I had something that would work. That was the beginning, the easy part, but in order to make productive business from this endeavor where I could make a small profit, I knew I had to get set up with an office space, which included a computer and office supplies before I was ready to start building an inventory. The computer was a struggle and presented in a language that was worse than foreign to me, but fortunately I could touch type, which was the first hurdle. But those early computers were not very user friendly and caused me to scream often and tear my hair out in frustration as I gradually mastered the wild thing, which was only achieved with the help of the patient Richard, to whom I give thanks, but although he was considerably ahead of my ability to understand how the machine worked, he was still only a two-fingered typist. I stayed in contact with the original galleries and was able to persuade them to forward me the information about their supplier. It turned out to be the same supplier for each of them, not really a surprise. I researched and found that the largest supplier was a family-run company that owned most of all the original copper plates that were available, and that the business had been in the same family for two hundred years. A variety of every conceivable subject was available in their inventory, from seventeenth and eighteenth century London city scenes to those of tranquil rustic England, with sheep and thatched cottages from the same period. Also available were famous battle scenes taken from a variety of skirmishes the Brits had on the European continent during the same period and also marine seascapes, beautiful old sailing ships and portraiture of notable nobs from the last three hundred plus years, and many more unusual subjects. In those days when an artist had been engaged to execute a painting for a patron, it was, of course, a one off. But the art of engraving was very old and the old printmaking method was developed during the fifteenth century when metal plates began to replace the use of carved wooden printing blocks for the reproduction of works of art. This was also an art in its own right. The technique used to produce a hand-colored restrike engraving from the original plate is long and involved and requires many different labor intensive processes. The copper or steel plate has to be meticulously prepared by a highly skilled engraver who uses a variety of special tools that essentially haven't changed in design for hundreds of years. A very special high quality paper of a certain weight is made exclusively for this process in Scotland and the richness of inking in intaglio prints sets this method apart from all other print-making techniques. The finished results represent some of the finest traditional art prints available today, being true archival quality etchings and engravings taken from the original steel and copper plates, printed on custom made acid free paper and then hand colored by artists using special ink compatible with the colors of the original painting. I could not resist surrounding myself with a large variety of these beautiful prints, it felt as if I had a display of all aspects of English life and history in every room of my home, and I loved that. The secret to the success of the company I was to deal with was their large production set-up. Owning almost all the available plates it was in their interest to keep them in a healthy and viable print-worthy state so they limited the number of times any one plate was available for use; this preserved the original engravers cuts into the copper surface and extended the life of the plate and the whole process. I was invited to buy from this company, a real privilege since I only bought selectively and did not have a huge inventory. It was a pleasure to do business with this old and respected family. They were also, and remain, an honorable family company who I found to be the most dignified people one could ever have the pleasure of doing business with, and even though I was considered a small dealer, they always treated me with the utmost respect. I did, however, have the nerve to call my home-based company the British Collection, which, with the accent, went down well and opened many doors for me in those areas of Boston I had targeted and I managed to make a reasonable amount of pocket money while acquiring many happy "word of mouth" patrons. I found a sensitive reliable framer in Newton who was an artist in his own right and so instinctively understood the value of the prints that I brought to him to frame, and we always discussed and mutually agreed on the choice of matt and frame for each piece I presented to him. With everything in place and functioning, I used another idea to get my prints a wider audience, and I made connections with a number of Boston's most respected galleries and arranged for them to sell for me on consignment basis. I then rotated the prints regularly so they always looked fresh in which ever gallery they were placed. It was good for them because there was no initial outlay or risk, and I was offering an imported high-quality, very attractive, well-priced art of genuine value for which they made a small percentage when selling the piece and I would make the larger percentage for owning it. I don't know how I found the time with the busy schedule I already juggled, but somehow I did and it was fun and I could work it around my singing commitments while making myself some pocket money, which I needed.

In the meantime I had music scores to memorize, rehearsals to attend, recordings to make, concerts to perform, voice lessons to take seriously and a family to watch over. I was happy to be busy. This was the summer of 1984 and Tanglewood was also beckoning close on the horizon with preparations to be made and new works to be learnt. But I also needed to pay attention to matters on the home front. My daughter was half way through her degree at McGill and was thoroughly enjoying the stimulation of college life especially in an interesting city in a "foreign" country. She continued to do well both in her college courses and with her health. There were only occasional and oblique references to the accident. Mostly she was engrossed in the learning experience in Montreal and having fun at the same time. Beth had also started to volunteer in the neurological ward at the university hospital where her curiosity may have had some connection to her own injuries, hopefully helping her to come to terms by learning more about the subject, and I was glad.

She then decided to change her major to neurobiology and was exposed to some interesting information on new medical research in the field and most of the breakthrough science was coming from the very research led by her professors at McGill. All the major papers and books on the subject were being written by the professors in her department. I could tell how excited she was about this and was very happy for her having found a subject she felt passionate about and perhaps it helped her on another level, to understand intellectually what had happened to her as a result of the accident. I am only speculating because it was never discussed. And so in her second year, she decided to shift her major from chemistry to neurobiology, and her passion for the subject never wavered. I needed to drive to Canada to fetch her home at the beginning and end of the school year, which also gave me an opportunity to have time to myself and listen in the car to the study choral tapes given us for memorization of the next concert piece. Beth had made many friends and was renting a small 'pad' off campus, glad to be away from the institutional rules of the college dorm. She loved Montreal and it was fun to visit her and take the various tours she had planned, helping us practice our French and familiarize ourselves with the attractive and interesting city. Andrew, who still had two more years of high school, was also making good grades and enjoying his school, becoming quite an athlete when pushed, and he continued to entertain everyone in his family and many friends alike. He was very musically inventive, accompanying himself on the piano and guitar as he produced his own "original" songs, which he sang with a warm, sonorous baritone voice much to everyone's enjoyment. Some of his friends also had instruments and they loved to "jam" together frequently in the big living room with the wooden fireplace. It was great to listen to and I felt very good about the rest of the guys being Andrew's friends. They all went on to study and became professionals in their own field of dreams as well as committed life-long friends, seemingly unmarred by their teenage antics.

Richard was director of Strategic Planning with GTE and enjoying the stimulation of his work along with the associations he made especially with Dr. John Redmond who encouraged him in his efforts to get many of his papers in the field relating to the management of the technology published. He began to make a wider name for himself on his subject and was asked to represent the company by joining an organization called the Industrial Research Institute, which was made up of business heads of research and development who met frequently to discuss movement in this important and necessary field. Very soon he was heading up important committee meetings and became an acknowledged expert and a sought after speaker on the subject and soon rocketed to his own form of stardom and I was pleased and proud for him.

While the grand old Symphony Hall in Boston was the solid home base of the BSO and where the chorus spent the vast majority of its time for most of the year, a palpable excitement began in early June as hearts and minds began to shift perspective and thoughts as all preparations began to shift west, to the beautiful Berkshire Hills and the small elegant towns of Lennox, Massachusetts, home of the hugely popular Red Lion Inn, and a few miles away the equally endearing Stockbridge. There was a mass musical exodus both mentally and physically from the city to the quiet peace and natural beauty of the Berkshires, where making music took on a whole new meaning. There had been musical musings in the area for many decades, and to quote Peggy Daniels in her lovely book about Tanglewood, "The Berkshire Symphonic

Festival Incorporated, a pioneer organization in the field of music, got its start in 1934-a worrying time when the future was heavily clouded." Regardless, a rallying cry had gone out to an already enthusiastic local group who felt that there could be few things more enchanting than listening to a great symphony orchestra playing music on a sublime summer evening, under the moon and stars.

With such inspired courage and against an increasingly grim backdrop of potential international woes and dangers that were brewing, this small group persevered and refused to allow the terrors of the time to interfere with their plans. Against a backdrop of rapidly rising unemployment, causing stress and tension within the United States, while Adolph Hitler and the Nazis were breathing menacing fire in Europe. But musicians and lovers of music everywhere know that especially in times of stress, whether personal or national, beautiful music can deeply soothe the troubled heart and mind. Following a marathon fund-raising effort organized by a dedicated and determined group of wealthy patrons in the area along with the enthusiastic and essential services of unemployed carpenters, electricians, plumbers, and general laborers from the Berkshire towns of Stockbridge, Lee, and Lennox, the big event took shape, and the patrons would be able to sit in a newly constructed open-air amphitheater. To allow the listener unlimited opportunities for the fanciful flight of his imagination and the comfort of the body, all the lights would be turned off at the commencement of the concert—the moon, by way of reassurance, would be full for the duration of all performances! And so a great tradition began on August 23, 1934, with the moon shining in full splendor, although briefly, above the new amphitheater, but with the stars reliably twinkling, refusing to miss a note of the music, along with the many sponsors who had made good on their promise of bringing the dream to fruition during such challenging times.

Dr. Henry Hadley, a noted conductor-composer of the period and a major organizer behind the idea and event, supplied the orchestra of sixty-four men from the New York Philharmonic, and on cue lifted his baton to open the first performance with Berlioz's lively "Overture" Carnival Romain. There were three thousand people in the audience! Clearly the great idea was launched and off to a good start that would have a very promising future.

"We believe that music is one art. The chorus, the symphony orchestra, the virtuoso, recitalist, and the string quartet are not competitive "attractions" for the public fashion in patronage, but are instruments of a single craft with similar responsibilities" (Robert Shaw, *A Choral Creed*).

Singing is the most direct expression of music, and singing was to be very much a part of Serge Koussevitzky's master plan. The maestro knew Robert Shaw and decided at that time he was the right man for Tanglewood and he even gave him his first opportunity to conduct the symphony orchestra and Shaw went on to spend three fruitful seasons there helping to put together the first Tanglewood chorus of only twenty-two singers, before he moved on to inspire many other choruses and form his own Robert Shaw Chorale. For many years after that the choruses were mostly pick-up affairs using Music Center vocal students and local college singers but in 1970 the Boston Symphony Orchestra, which had taken the reigns decided it needed a permanent year-round chorus, a notion that most American orchestras do not entertain because it's much easier to hire a local group when needed and avoid the costs and logistical problems inherent in a full-time symphonic chorus. They asked John Oliver to form the Tanglewood Festival Chorus. John had been a student at the Berkshire Music Center himself before he went on to coach the vocal students, and for several years, John Oliver had also run the whole vocal program at the Berkshire Music Center. He chose the name of the chorus himself to give the ensemble a separate identity from that of the BSO. John's mode of operation followed Shaw's theories about singing: "The notion that you could put together a group of really great singers and somehow, by working together and singing intelligently, they would make a chorus without personally giving up those special individual vocal qualities which they possessed and which they brought to each performance."

And so in 1992, as a full member of this amazing organization and armed with the vocal tools of my trade, having completed my first orchestra season in the city, I set off for the beautiful Berkshires on my first exciting summer singing with the Tanglewood Festival Chorus.

I was not prepared for the reaction as I approached the large wrought-iron gates, passed the ticket booths where early throngs of people gently jostled one another. Their objective was to get as close to the front of the lawn and so nearer the amphitheater for a better view of the performers as possible, balancing their elaborate picnic supplies carefully to that end. Of course, the chorus had another entrance, but I wanted to get there early and explore everything before the warm-up. As I walked through the gates onto the Tanglewood grounds, the beauty of the scene before me immediately brought a broad and uncontrollable smile that spread across my lips and face and continued until I was tingling all over with excitement.

A bright green velvet carpet of fresh grass spread spaciously in front of me. The grounds' five hundred acres are spread across two former privately owned estates, one parcel of the land extended down to the shores of the Stockbridge Bowl and a great place to cool off if we had any spare time. One of the properties was formerly owned by William Tappan. It had a little red house on it which was rented out to Nathaniel Hawthorne and his family in the summer months of 1850. It was where Hawthorne wrote *The*

House of Green Gables and a childhood anthology of short stories called *The Tanglewood Tales*. Tappen loved Hawthorne's literary creation and named his property "Tanglewood," a name fondly embraced by all who have been acquainted with the special place. Inside the grounds to the left of the main gate stood the huge Koussevitsky Memorial Shed, the auditorium, looking unconventionally stark in such a setting. It could not be described as beautiful with its packed mud flooring, open sides, hard uncomfortable flip-up seating and strategically positioned steel posts bolted to the floor which reached high up to the roof, holding it up. I never thought it graced the landscape exactly but it worked. Patrons could sit and feel the breezes and watch the magnificent old trees swaying in time to the music.

Koussevitsky had wanted a simple but beautiful music pavilion to enhance the musical experience and to capture and embrace the out of doors. He asked a famous Finnish architect of the day to oblige, but the architect foolishly came in way over budget, so a compromise was reached from the suggestion of the local resident engineer Joseph Franz whose solution was to "build a simple, but functional 'shed' without walls, where the audience can enjoy seeing the lovely landscape while listening to the music." From the air the shed, which resembled a large piano, seated an audience of 5,200, while the surrounding lawn has been known to accommodate up to 10,000 more music lovers, many of whom bring their white table cloths, silver candelabras, and good cutlery and tuck into cold chicken, cool wine, and sweet little delicacies as they picnic under the stars. But God is certainly in the details. He did provide the "shed" with the most important gift of all—once it was in use it was found to be an amazing masterpiece of acoustical design.

Open on one side, the rustic wooden barn transformed into a rehearsal studio served us well, and we grew comfortably fond of the space. Our rehearsal place was a pleasant stroll from the main shed across the huge lawn and tucked away from the paths, the crowds of people and the main action, nestling in its own quiet little corner. As part of the Berkshire Music Center, the grounds were studded with many such interesting wooden structures, and unlike the shed, they blended beautifully with the landscape and were used by the students and faculty of the Berkshire Music Center. The Berkshire Music Center attracted and invited the finest group of international students to spend a summer under the tutorage of soloists from the orchestra and from visiting soloists from all over the world who were also engaged to perform in recitals and as part of the orchestral performances.

We would gather in the quiet, still mornings for rehearsals, carrying cups of tea or coffee into our small wooden rehearsal space, which opened onto a lawn with trees and an audience of birds who were sometimes in delightful competition with our vocal warm-up exercises. We would also meet there for the final warm-up an hour before a performance, this time with a handful of interested and devoted patrons gathering on the lawn in front of us and who loved to hear John Oliver put us through our paces, making sure that everything about our performance would be perfect, ensuring that our review by the music critic Richard Dyer in the next day's *Boston Globe* would be glowing.

Then would follow an experience I savored on every occasion. Together with a few friends we would begin to weave our way in our long white concert attire toward the shed for our on stage line-up. We made our way through the flickering candles and past the lawn audience sitting on their blankets enjoying a picnic, quietly sipping cool wine in relaxed anticipation for the performance that was to come. From the early days in the Berkshires, there had always been an expectation of respectable attire at these events and it was still generally adhered to, and so it was relaxed, smart but comfortable. As we floated through the huge and eager crowd a quiet murmur arose and began to grow and spread over the vast lawn as the audience whispered among themselves until it became speech, and then they nudged each other and strained their necks for a glimpse of our approaching, and as we picked our way through their ranks, we could hear words of warmth, of encouragement, of praise, and of appreciation and we smiled deeply as we heard the collective chant "Here come the Tanglewood Festival Chorus!"

Once lined up in our assigned positions we quietly made our way backstage through the hallways, passing orchestra members using their last few minutes before the performance to tune up their instruments and practice a tricky passage before they also were called to go on stage. We filed on stage and took up our positions on the risers behind the orchestra pit. We mostly sang in eight-part harmony depending on the musical format and we also sang "hashed," a term meaning that our voice parts were mixed together giving more nuance and a warmer blend to our voices, so we settled into our position beside our chorus friends, tenor or bass on one side, alto one or two on the other with another soprano further down the line. Ninety percent of the time we were without the prop of the music score having memorized the piece during our own periods of free time between rehearsals. Mostly we enjoyed the freedom from having to hold a heavy score throughout a long performance, but it meant that all eyes were fixed hypnotically on the conductor, and usually it was Maestro Ozawa who may have had a photographic memory and expected us to have the same. His energy and passion for the piece was also reflected in his sometimes wild physicality on the podium as he swayed his body and flashed his baton and along with his deeply penetrating eyes stared at us through an unruly mop of straight, black hair, he demanded contact with each individual member of the chorus, making our performance to both exciting and occasionally a little unnerving at the same time; certainly we were all very much engaged! Svengali, like he often had us willingly under his power and sometimes, we felt it caused us to sing in a hypnotic state! Yes, each performance took us to another place, a place we were all willing to be taken!

1986 was an eventful year for the family. Andrew graduated from Newton North High School and Beth graduated from McGill, in Montreal so there were many parties rejoicing in the accomplishments of both grown up children. I didn't think either of them needed or felt any pressure to make quick decisions about their immediate future and they deserved some time to relax and take stock before they decided what was best for them to do next. Andrew was quite happy to enter the University of Massachusetts campus, which had an excellent reputation at that time as being the best that the country's state university system had to offer, and he hoped to major in American history, which seemed an excellent fit for him. Beth relaxed also having clearly had an extraordinary experience at McGill, but there was something on her mind. Both of them caught up on their sleep, raided the refrigerator, and reunited with old friends who were also emerging from their studies at faraway places and the house became what it had always been, a favorite gathering place and the old party porch also resumed its function. The piano was still in tune and the house smiled at all the noise and activity that had returned. But within a week Beth made an announcement. She had decided to move to London. She planned to stay with family friends and relatives at first, find a job, and then live on her own. At first I was surprised and a little sad that she wanted to leave so soon but happy that she wanted to return to the city of her birth, recognizing it as the place she wanted to live and, for the first time, really discover. Andrew still had four years of college to contemplate before he was free to travel, and it was very obvious that he would miss Beth a great deal; he was also very envious. "We can all come and visit you," I declared, trying to be upbeat and genuinely thinking how possible that it would be and already planning my own trip while encouraging Andrew to embrace the idea, but he went very quiet as if he was already missing his sister. I also thought that Beth didn't want to stay in Boston and be reminded of the difficult experience she had been through and that she was concerned that I would take up the worrying mother role again and hover around her whenever I could. It made me sad but I also could understand and respected her need for space and separation and independence. I also wanted to ask Beth questions regarding her welfare but sensed that it was the last thing she wanted to discuss, especially with me. What she was silently saying to me was "look how well I am, look how well I'm coping, look how many friends I have and how much fun I am having." But she was smoking a lot of cigarettes, which worried me. Parenting was not for the faint hearted, but then it never was and the important thing was to stay as close and as interested in their activities and their wellbeing as possible, while appearing not to be, for fear of being given the dreaded label of an overprotective mother. In total Beth would spend thirteen years away, first in Montreal and then, almost immediately in London for another nine years. She was brave and determined to make her own way and claim London as her own, understanding and sharing with us the many of joys of the city that I had loved so much and which I still missed. I physically and emotionally missed her a great deal and so did her father, but she did write wonderful long letters to me describing her walks and wanderings, discovering and revisiting those places I used to talk about as if she wanted to follow my footsteps on the pavements where I had also walked when I was her age, all of which brought me great solace. She visited the old concert halls and galleries, walked in the many lovely parks, admired the architecture everywhere, and went to as many plays and concerts as money would allow. She had a job in the bustling, colorful theatre district working in a famous old pub, which boasted many unusual characters as patrons among its clientele who were drawn from the surrounding theatre area. The old Victorian Sailsbury Public House also had a display of beautiful cut glass windows and mirrors, which had to be removed during the German 'Blitz on London in 1940–41 when London was bombed by the Luftwaffe every night for 246 nights, from September 7, 1940, to May 10, 1941. Many great buildings were pulverized into dust and so to save the millions of treasures large and small from all over the city they were stored for safe keeping in faraway secret places until after the war when they were all happily returned to their original homes–that is if they were still standing.

    By this time Andrew was pleading with us to let him join Beth, which meant putting his college history studies on hold, but he needed to be part of this adventure and it would be a great learning experience for him as well, especially while his sister was also there and could watch out for him. Within a few months Andrew had joined her and I felt very happy that they were enjoying this adventurous time together. London is a great walking city and they explored and discovered all the gems that I and their father had suggested, and they found others for themselves, peeling back the multi layers of the city's history street by street, making old and new connections for themselves, and in the process, they also came to know my favorite streets and the out-of- the-way haunts that only a local knows. Both of them, born Londoners, they easily and quickly became locals themselves and to use a favorite expression of all London taxi drivers, it would be a compliment to say "they got the knowledge". They also sought out and reunited with their long-lost cousins and other family members and discovered some of their own history including the places where they had both been born and the streets where they had lived. They explored the area and street where I lived and grew up until I left as a young woman, first to be married and then, a few years later, with the little family in my arms making the journey to America. I remember hearing Beth telling the story of our journey to America as she witnessed the event. This is close to how she and I remembered it: "That was when we all left on a long train from a big station called Waterloo in London, waving goodbye to Granddad Garside who couldn't keep up with the moving train and was crying."

Andrew was having a great time. It was party time every night in the Sailsbury, but over the period of the year he spent working in the London pub certain things became obvious to him. Most of the other people he worked with had no other skills and he could see that bar work was a dead-end job. It was fine and fun for a student to make some extra cash between semesters, but a demoralizing disaster if you had no other options and there were many dropouts around who had few options open to them and would be forced to take on casual work for the rest of their lives unless they decided to get an education. Probably for many different reasons, sadly many chose not to, and remained in a low-pay work rut for most of their lives. However, it was not difficult to find help filling in the educational gaps in England particularly in the big cities where there were many schools and junior colleges designed for this exact purpose, at very low cost. But for Andrew, who had many natural talents, this was a very useful evaluation for him to make by himself, without parental interference or persuasion. In a mature way he began to realize that he should start to take seriously his own educational ambitions and do what needed to be done to get his own university degree. He had seen how bleak life looked without a higher education; it was very limited indeed. His experience in England had been great; but he needed and wanted to come back to Boston and go through the process of applying to university. In 1988 Andrew started his history studies in earnest on the Boston campus of the University of Massachusetts.

Beth remained in London but like Andrew discovered very soon that she also wanted to explore her own employment possibilities in a more serious setting and hopefully put her shiny new degree in neurobiology into good use. She interviewed and was accepted at the Institute of Ophthalmology doing research on the eye-brain connection, and where a breakthrough technique called patch clamping helped provide exciting results, which were very important to the work she did there over the next four years and resulted in her obtaining a PhD. She was paid a pittance but it was enough for her to share a flat with some other young people all of them positive but struggling and propping each other up in many ways while trying to make ends meet. But what kept her completely engaged was the importance of her research work.

It was great to have Andrew at home again. We were within a reasonable commute to UMass and so he lived at home, which was convenient and made all of us very happy. I frequently heard the old piano being played in the living room when he was around, and I enjoyed a sense of contentment and pleasure knowing that the last few years had been good to all of us, and we had all recovered physically and emotionally from a few challenging years.

The New England spring was a definite challenge. It was my

birthday month and March proved to be as frustrating and challenging as usual—where in England spring is abundant with color, even as early as February little flowers are everywhere. March here would often bring the largest snow fall of the year and the possibility of a large storm was on everyone's mind. But for me, this was going to be a big, milestone birthday—I was to be fifty years old! Some plans had been tentatively made for a slap-up dinner somewhere, or a small party. Certainly a bash of some kind was in order, I thought. But the dreariness of the still long, dark days produced an inertia everyone living in the state.

A few days before my birthday when I was glad to have mealtime over and the kitchen cleaned up, I was looking forward to curling up with some interesting television to watch, always a challenge, when the front door bell rang. Who on earth could it be, I thought, slightly irked by the interruption, and wondering why anyone would come calling on such a cold dark night, disturbing me just as I was settling in for the evening. I reluctantly dragged myself to the front door. It was too dark to see who was standing on the top step. I opened the first door and then opened the large front door. I stared dumbly at the person in front of me, all wrapped up in hat, scarf, coat, and boots, and it took me several long seconds to believe what I thought I saw. I must be wrong, I thought. Feeling embarrassed, I hesitated before I spoke, "You look like my daughter Beth," but my mind was telling me it can't be Beth. She would have called; anyway she is in London. But Beth was not in London; she was standing on the top step and speaking to me. "Hello, Mum—surprise, surprise! Happy Birthday, I am your big birthday present!" I was blinking back annoying tears while shaking with shock and joy and amazement. "Why are you here? What's wrong? Are you all right? Why didn't you let me know you were coming?" I rambled on, by which time she was in my arms, giving me one of the most memorable hugs I believe I had ever had. I didn't realize I was crying until I couldn't see because of the tears, by which time Richard and Andrew were by my side and we were all laughing and crying together. This has to be the best surprise and best well-kept secret of all time and certainly the very best birthday present any mother could ever receive. Richard's secret plan had been in the works for some time and I never had the slightest idea—sneaky, lovely husband, he definitely deserved the Best Husband of the Year Award for this oh so memorable and over-the-top surprise!

We enjoyed a good, stimulating, and even exciting life with lots of interesting friends, places to visit at home and abroad, a house always full of people young and old, which generated much laughter and great conversation. I was blessed to have such a warm and welcoming house that everyone enjoyed, in the summertime on the party porch - off the elegant vestibule with its cool original terracotta tile floor, which felt so perfect under bare feet, and in the wintertime around the roaring log fire blazing in the middle of the splendid old fireplace watching as my Westie, Josephine, edged onto her favorite spot on the rug not wanting to miss anything that was going on, and listening with her pricked ears to Andrew picking out a tune from his inventive repertoire, always ready to entertain the admiring crowd, including dogs, on the good old Yamaha. I suppose one can become a little complacent at times imagining that our lives would continue like this indefinitely–I felt more settled than I had in many years and I didn't want anything to change. I had had more than my share of change! My singing with the BSO would always be with me, my print business was a small but viable enterprise, both children were happy and doing well and Richard's name was well known and growing beyond his company. His company– well yes, changes were happening there—was changing its name from GTE to Verizon and some reshuffling was to be expected. While Richard felt relatively safe, as safe as you can in the American corporate jungle, he was also thinking that it might be a good idea to see what other possibilities were out there. Then an amazing thing happened, completely out of the blue, something that was about to turn our lives around again in a very unusual and wonderful way. Richard was called to Washington DC!

CHAPTER FIVE
PART ONE

Called To Serve

It might have been difficult to predict what happened next and yet it was not an improbable outcome. Once you connected all the dots, it was, indeed, an obvious one, although it was a very different development from the one we had been expecting. Richard's close involvement with the Industrial Research Institute went back more than a decade, first as professional representative for GTE and eventually as a member of the IRI Board of Directors. Most of the members of the IRI headed up the R and D departments of their companies and shared their professional views, and successes with each other. Over several years, he published many papers on industrial research and development and related strategies for growth and spoke frequently to academic, business schools, and professional groups. An immediate connection came when Richard met Dr. Ann Harris, and it formed a relationship that led to many years of positive professional collaboration between the two of them. It was a phone call on that dreary spring evening that set into action the course of our lives for the next four and an half years. It was from Ann Harris.

THE RELUCTANT IMMIGRANT

In January 1993, a young, forty-six-year-old Democrat from the southern state of Arkansas was inaugurated as president of the United States in Washington DC. I was not paying particular attention at that time to all things political and he was not a well-known name to us, but that would soon change as we began to take notice of the changing political scene.

He was especially bright with an impressive array of degrees from the top Ivy League Universities, including one from Georgetown University, where he was a member of Phi Beta Kappa. He had also earned a Rhode's Scholarship to attend the great old English University of Oxford where he excelled in many areas including the art of debate. He was married to an attractive and ambitious woman, equally gifted in scholarship and someone who could easily match and beat him on any subject in debate at any time. Both of them received their law degrees from Yale Law School. Politics was a natural calling for both the Clintons, and they each entertained broad ambitions, which made them a formidable, a very powerful, and attractive duo. As the governor of the state of Arkansas from 1983 to 1992, William Jefferson "Bill" Clinton would inevitably meet Dr. Ann Harris. A chemist, she had received a BS and PhD degrees from the Universities of Arkansas, but Dr. Harris shone in many ways. She had already acquired an international reputation in the scientific community and was the first woman to be appointed to high office by Presidents Jimmy Carter's and Ronald Reagan's holding office twice on the Board of the National Science Foundation in both their administrations and again on the Council of Advisors on Science and Technology for President Herbert Walker Bush.

Each government department or agency was structured in the same way and headed by a secretary with the assistants in charge of the many and various sub-departments within the agency, with all of them reflecting and focusing on different aspects of the president's platform for the country's future going forward, which in this vital case was commerce. Comprising twelve different agencies, the mission of the Department of Commerce is very broad. It is essentially responsible for helping to make the many aspects of American business more innovative at home and more competitive abroad and in so doing positively touching the lives of Americans every day.

The new United States Secretary of Commerce was a tall, handsome, very charismatic African American who was also a persuasive speaker, well acquainted with the right people, and he knew his way around the Washington political scene. He was the first African American to hold this position, and he came with his own wealth of credentials. Raised in New York in a middle-class family, he demonstrated at an early age a desire to become involved in community action and soon belonged to many social and philanthropic organizations in the city. He was the first African American member of the all-male collegiate fraternity Sigma Phi Epsilon at Middlebury College, and after graduating, he joined the army and served in South Korea and in Europe. Discharged in 1967 Ron Brown joined a leading economic equality group in the United States, the National Urban League, rising to Deputy Executive Director, and soon after, he also received a law degree from St. John's University. Becoming more involved in politics, he worked on the campaign of Senator Edward Kennedy who was seeking the party's presidential nomination in 1979 and shortly thereafter as a lawyer and lobbyist, running Jesse Jackson's campaign in 1988. A year later he was elected chairman of the Democratic National Committee and in 1992 played an integral part in running both the convention and in the successful bid for the Presidency of Bill Clinton. Ron Brown was very popular and he was well equipped in many areas, which would prove indispensable in this important new role as Secretary of Commerce.

It would not be long before an announcement would be made by President Bill Clinton's new administration, and it would be for Dr. Ann Harris to act as Under Secretary for Technology, for the Technology Administration in the Department of Commerce, reporting directly to Ron Brown. The process of vetting and vetoing already excellent candidates for various high level positions continued, but there was one person, for one position where all concerned agreed that the fit was perfect. The important position waiting to be filled at the United States Commerce Department was for the Assistant Secretary of Commerce and that was why Ann Harris was about to call Richard Neville, who, completely unaware of these events, found himself to be in the right place at the right time, waiting in the wings back in Boston when the phone rang!

Even though they had been colleagues and friends for many years, it was still a very big surprise for Richard when he received the call from Ann Harris. A very happy and exciting surprise and as he described the details to me, I could tell he was moved, for he also understood what an honor this opportunity was and expressed how humbled he felt by being called to serve. He spent the night pacing and thinking everything through and called Dr. Harris early next morning accepting the position. There was much to accomplish, and she needed him to start immediately on the understanding that for a short period he would be the acting assistant secretary until such time as the Senate met, considered, and approved his appointment officially. With that, he hit the ground running, leaving Boston within a few days to join Dr. Harris as they began the non-stop meetings that were required for all involved during this vital transition period of the administration, that needed all their agencies to be staffed and up and running as soon as possible with their agendas set in place and with their hand-picked personnel organized to take over.

There was no time for a farewell party. I had to stay in Boston to sell the house and dismantle my life one more time. The house selling was made extremely easy for me, and I managed everything without the need of realtor. I have described the house and location earlier. That it was within a leisurely stroll of a synagogue made it even more desirable, and the house was sold to a delighted couple known to our neighbors who had eyed and longed for the property for years. I was happy with the price and they were happy that we could vacate the house within a few weeks, so all that was left for me to do was to organize the moving company. Richard was immersed in his new position and wouldn't be able to get back to Boston, but I changed my mind about a party and decided to have one last big bash for myself, to say good-bye to each room in my house and to my many singing colleagues and the friends I'd made from my print business and all the others I had gathered up along the Boston way. All the while my head was filled with great expectation, and although I was by this time very experienced at pulling up my roots, saying sad farewells, and leaving one life behind in exchange for a new one, I was still in wonder at the way in which one's life can so quickly change, the nature of change, and the demands both welcome and unwelcome that must inevitably accompany that change. In this case I took on those demands willingly. I was going to Washington DC, the nation's capital city, and I was happy to be going on my husband's coat tails and was sure that this would be a good change and a memorable experience for both of us, and I was very, very excited to begin this new adventure.

The Industrial Research Institute had its headquarters conveniently positioned in Washington DC, and we knew many of the people who staffed the organization and had considered them old friends of many years. When they heard the news of Richard's new position as Assistant Secretary for Commerce, they were thrilled for him, and congratulations flooded in from many people and places across the country. The friendly staff of the IRI wanted to wine and dine us and take us under their wing and advise us where to live and where to shop and where to eat. I was even invited by one well- meaning lady for lunch at the Four Seasons mostly to be instructed on how I should behave as the wife of an Assistant Secretary, which at first I thought to be rather unnecessary and I was somewhat disdainful and scoffed at the notion, but I realized very soon that I had been given some useful advice that might be very helpful in my own new public role. And so I was polite and gracious and felt completely at ease by the challenge, believing even before the instruction began that I could competently handle any social situation I found myself in. I regarded that having been an IRI wife for many years, I had been schooled in the social arts having had many social demands come my way within the various activities of the IRI both in the United States and abroad. I had been well trained over a number of years and knew how to shake hands, use a napkin, not drink too much or talk too much or too loudly (and not in any way say *anything* negative about the good old US of A or anything that could embarrass the president and lastly not to use any of my favorite English expletives), and so very soon I felt confident and comfortable that I would be perfectly acceptable even in the company of my queen (although I would refuse to curtsy), let alone the president of the United States! Besides, I had an added virtue. I had been brought up with impeccable old-school English manners. I still had an enviable English accent, which would open any door, and I ate with both a knife and a fork!

Gentle, premature pressure was being put on us to buy a house in Georgetown because it was where all the action was and it was an easy commute for Richard to the Commerce Department. But until he was formally confirmed, which would make his appointment permanent and official, we preferred to rent an apartment in the center of Georgetown at the Georgetown Suites situated close to all the action. I was excited to explore my new town and a convenient, close-by daily stroll from our apartment took my obedient West Highland Terrier Josephine and me down beside the quiet C and O (Chesapeake and Ohio) canal where we could walk along the tow path and watch and wave at the tourists taking a leisurely ride on the now rustic barges as they took a slow glide past us. Originally in the eighteenth century, Georgetown was a slave-trading center, but it was also a key player at that time in what was called the economy's life-blood—the tobacco trade—and the barges would be piled high with bales of tobacco being carried westward, on their way to Ohio.

Georgetown is now considered the most desirable of destinations, but during the early and middle of the nineteenth century, it fell on very hard times with the decline of the C and O trade, which came with the inevitable development of railroads. Georgetown soon became a run-down, smelly, industrial town with one of Washington's worst slum problems. It was happily rescued in the 1930s when it was rediscovered and rehabilitated by officials of Roosevelt's New Deal. In the 1960s, it was rediscovered all over again when President Kennedy's administration made it their headquarters and an enclave that became nationally known for a glittering lifestyle with chic dinner parties where very important people gathered to make very important decisions. But I was getting carried away, back to Georgetown later. What I was most interested in exploring was the bigger city of the capitol itself. Washington kept calling me to explore and there was so much I wanted to know about its history and I had to acknowledge it first.

With my guide book in my hand I took off for Washington DC (District of Columbia). With its beautiful white buildings it is known the world over as a very attractive spacious city full of attractive and interesting buildings, impressive monuments, and wonderful museums set alongside handsome tree-lined boulevards—it was all that and more. The original design was laid out by the Frenchman Pierre L'Enfant who left his native France because he was sympathetic toward the Americans' fight in the

Revolutionary War and wanted to join its forces and help fight the Brits. From an obscure beginning he became the trusted city planner for George Washington, designing the city from what was then a district of hills, forests, marshes, and plantations, an area measuring approximately one hundred square miles. L'Enfant envisioned a grand capital city with a Congress House at the top of the highest hill with a commanding view of the future capital city, a place he told Washington was "a pedestal waiting for a super structure." Construction of the Capitol building began in 1793 when President Washington laid the buildings' cornerstone. The huge, twin-shelled iron dome that you now see, because it is the tallest and most prominent aspect of the building, was not, however, completed until 1863. Lincoln, who was now the president, oversaw its completion as a necessary deed for the survival of the Union. The statue on top of the Capitol dome is called Freedom and was cast from a plaster model that sculptor Thomas Crawford made in Italy. Freedom's head was originally covered by a Phrygian cap, which was an ancient symbol of freed slaves, who used a simple cloth covering to hide their shaved heads.

Before Lincoln was assassinated, he had managed to garner just enough votes from Congress to end the scourge of slavery, but the Secretary of War at the time was Jefferson Davis, and the future president of the Confederacy, and he was not exactly a fan of slaves ever being liberated, even symbolically, and pressure was put on the architect who was compelled to replace the Phrygian cap for a crested Roman battle helmet, supposedly representing America's victory over tyranny. Funny they didn't see the hypocrisy there. Following a near sinking on the journey from Italy, the nineteen-foot statue was finally set in place in December 1863. And so despite the Civil War, Lincoln was successful in accomplishing his goal of completing the project, and it probably did help to keep the new Union together. At a time so fraught with uncertainty, symbols can become an inspiration. If you see the lantern just below Freedom lit, it means that the House or the Senate are all working overtime in a night session, which as we know, doesn't happen very often.

Back to L'Enfant's vision and the building of a spacious and beautiful capital city where there would be wide avenues, public squares, and inspiring buildings, the center piece being the great public walk, which today we refer to as the National Mall. It was designed to be a wide, straight strip of grass and trees that stretched from Capitol Hill to the Potomac River, a distance of approximately two miles. Included in the plan were to be the two lively and crucial port towns of Alexandria and Georgetown. Inspired by the topography of this rolling landscape at the confluence of two great rivers, the Frenchman envisioned and fashioned a city not only with flair but where important buildings would occupy places based on changes in the elevation and the contours of waterways. His design was based on European models translated to fit with American ideals. "The entire city was built around the idea that every citizen was equally important, and the Mall was designed to be an open space which would encourage its use by all of the people—a very egalitarian idea" according to L'Enfant's biographer Scott Berg. Also in keeping with the sentiment were Thomas Jefferson's wishes to make Washington an "American Paris" with "low and convenient buildings" built on "light and airy" streets.

Early on I fell in love with the whole area and visited frequently enjoying that airy feeling and the compatibility that each building demonstrated within its own space on the elegant National Mall. In the heat of Washington's three hot seasons, the cool white simplicity of the architectural grandeur of the buildings did not overpower the individual but instead would beckon and draw you inside. All the museums are easily accessible, and each echo with their outward harmony those perfect exhibits on display on the inside of each building, inviting visitors to explore a variety of some of the world's finest artifacts in the galleries and art museums. Sharing the space along the Mall with the great museums of art, there are just as many museums that are devoted to the acknowledgements of natural history and those that examine the accomplishments of the science, technology, and space. It was a collective "Mecca of Tributes" to mankind's great achievements.

Running parallel with the Mall is Constitution Avenue along which many handsome government buildings are built, broken up by the occasional restaurant, and on the corner of Constitution and Pennsylvania Avenues sits an attractive, white, and architecturally more modern building housing the Canadian Embassy, a place that I would visit frequently and come to have great affection for. Not to be outdone, at the opposite end on the corner of Constitution Avenue was the Department of Commerce where Richard was hard at work every day, doing the nation's business, having meetings in his office suite, with rarely any time to look out at the great view from his window where to the right on Pennsylvania Avenue he could see the White House and on the left the Washington Monument. The compatibility in building design over much of the city gave a spacious, orderly and uniform appearance to the wide streets, and I particularly enjoyed the unusual and attractive terracotta tiled façade placed on top of all the shallow roofing, giving a satisfying, and decorative unity to the overall style. Like the rings of a great tree, Washington's buildings and public spaces trace the American past, from the outer layers of the Watergate and the Vietnam Memorial down to the inmost bands of pre-revolutionary Georgetown and the Marine Barracks.

But the city's core has always been the White House, more modest by far than the mansions occupied by heads of state in many less affluent or powerful countries, but for more than two hundred years, it has been a strong symbol of America all over the world. The president's neighborhood is situated on Pennsylvania Avenue, in an area known as Lafayette Square, which was once a family farm, orchard, and burial ground when L'Enfant's plan projected it as the president's park, where the chief executive could relax and seek relief from the capital's sizzling summers. There sits the handsome, accessible but unassuming, gracious-looking residence, the home of the sitting president, also known as the Nation's House, and recognized affectionately by all as the White House.

In 1791 L'Enfant also selected the site for what would eventually become the tallest structure in Washington DC, the Washington Monument, and although there is no law requiring it, it is generally understood and accepted that all buildings stay below the height of the monument, which when it was finally erected stood at 550 feet. Considering it was to be built as recognition and a tribute to the nation's great founder and leader, there was certainly a lot of indecision and procrastinating involved in getting the project off the ground, so to speak. After much debate over where the money was going to come from for the project, which sounds familiar, the cornerstone was finally laid at an elaborate July 4 ceremony in 1848, but it wasn't dedicated until 1885 and finally opened to the public in October 1888, more than a hundred years since L'Enfant selected the site. Slow goings! It also must have seemed very sad "slow goings" for Monsieur L'Enfant himself, the mind behind the miracle plan, since he died in poverty, never having received payment for the work he spent years of his life executing for his adopted country, the fruits of which are enjoyed by the citizens of the city, country, and world today, hardly any of them giving him a thought.

I spent many solitary hours, never tiring, as I explored this great walking city. It is so open and inviting, and with its frequent water views, abundant green lawns and perfect trees positioned along small paths that meander gently, taking the willing walker in different directions of surprise and discovery, which often lead to a quiet, unexpected, and solemn moment spent beside a monument that is moving in its poignancy.

With some small help from Mr. Whitman's concise *Off the Beaten Track*, a little book I wish I'd had in my hands when first exploring my new home, he writes about Memorial Walk, an area that meanders across the National Mall, through the park and the polo fields, along the Potomac River and winds up at the Jefferson Memorial, and if you are lucky to be there during the season, you can see the lovely cherry blossom trees in bloom and reflected in the water of the Tidal Basin. Circular marble steps lead you to the nineteen-foot standing replica of Thomas Jefferson, one of the American founding fathers and the third president of the United States. The neo-classical building was designed by the architect John Russell Pope and construction, which was discussed over many years, wasn't completed until in 1947 when the finished bronze cast (statue) of Jefferson was positioned to stand under a shallow dome in the middle of a circular marble colonnade of ionic columns, open to the elements. On the panel of the southwest interior wall are excerpts from his famous and moving Declaration of Independence which he wrote in 1776.

At the end of the National Mall facing the national monument at one end and separated by the long rectangular reflecting pool stands another building influenced by the ancient Greeks. Approval and agreement over the existence and position and architects of the many monuments located on and around the National Mall took many decades and many presidents and much discussion and disagreement before there was any final consensus. But looking at the finished plan, so far, perhaps it was worth the wait. It is the magnificent and fitting marble statue by Daniel Chester French which symbolizes Abraham Lincoln's greatness, and I found that standing in front of this imposing work was a humbling experience, regardless of ones' country or origin, because it speaks to all people, everywhere. When you go on to read his solemn words of inspiration from the Gettysburg Address and his Second Inaugural Address sculpted into the walls one cannot help being deeply reflective and moved by them and ponder on how they still resonate today. His message is universal. The monument is filled with symbolism: the thirty-six columns represent the states in the union at the time of Lincoln's death by assassination, the forty-eight stone festoons on the attic above the columns represent the forty-eight states in 1922. Above each of the inscriptions is a sixty-by-twelve foot mural painted by Jules Guerin graphically portraying the governing principles evident in Lincoln's life, they being Freedom, Liberty, Immortality, Justice, Law, Fraternity, and Charity. Those words and the moral stature of the man have made the Memorial a symbolic, sacred venue especially for the civil rights movement. The memorial continues to be a rallying point for movements of protest and civil rights. Denied an audience in 1939 by the conservative group called the Daughters of the American Revolution, the famous African-American contralto Marion Anderson with the defiant help of Eleanor Roosevelt, transferred her performance to the steps of the Lincoln Memorial where she performed in front of a live audience of seventy thousand. And it was in front of the reflecting pool and on those same steps in 1963 where Martin Luther King delivered his historic speech "I Have a Dream" before the memorial honoring the Emancipation president and his proclamation of one hundred years earlier. The Lincoln Memorial will always continue to be a rallying point for movements of protest and civil rights.

In a city full of worthy and moving monuments celebrating the short, important, and action-filled moments of the nation's history, I felt that the most poignant spot in Washington, however, was the Vietnam Veteran's Memorial. A competition was held nationwide for the most appropriate design, and at first, there was considerable angst and anger over the winner who was a young twenty-year-old female and Yale undergraduate who was born in this country of Chinese immigrants. Her name was Maya Ying Lin. She won over many hundreds of applicants, many of them already known and respected for their work and mostly male. There was an outcry of indignation for a multiple of reasons, ostensibly criticizing the design because, at first, it seemed so bleak and comfortless, but an on-going dark murmur of disapproval that I could not understand, continued for a variety of other reasons until the memorial was in place.

The nation was still emotionally raw over what had been the longest war in its history. The Vietnam War began in 1954 and didn't end until 1975. It was perhaps the most unpopular foreign war ever waged with huge losses on both sides, but once Maya Ying Lin's unusual design was built and in place, citizens flocked to give their respects and spill their grief. Her brilliance was in the stark simplicity of the design. Two long, low, triangular walls of reflective black granite were sunk into the ground at an angle of 125 degrees, with the earth forming a bank behind them. Onto these walls were etched the names of the fifty-eight thousand Americans who had died in that war. Hundreds of people visited daily, searching among the names for a friend or loved one, often with pencil and paper to trace an impression of a loved one's etched name. They placed flowers and small mementos along the length of the wall as they left, their wet cheeks joining the reflection of trees, lawns, flowers, and other monuments in the background. I also witnessed many wrenching, unresolved emotions evident among the crowd who were confronted by a huddled group of badly injured war veterans dispersed among them. Most of these vets were still dealing with the loss of friends and their own harsh injuries and had many unresolved emotions. Standing together in small groups or alone, these sad and disheveled, un-kept soldiers, half in uniform, half in old civilian clothes, angrily agonizing their personal pain both internally and externally at the indignation and fury over the loss of their comrades and the less than understanding official treatment they had received on their own return from hell. Mostly the public visitors to the Wall seemed emotionally confused, and I thought some seemed uncomfortable in the presence of these poor, often pot-smoking, scruffy men. I became a quiet observer and on many occasions would watch the sad scene for long periods, not because I was gawking but because it was bringing me a deeper understanding and perspective of American history and its people. These were the same people I brushed against daily in a hundred public places and where small pleasantries were exchanged on both sides, these always included a comment about my accent and my own home city. When I told them I was a citizen, not a visitor, there would always be an expression of surprise and pleasure in their eyes and on their lips.

Close by is the Memorial to the fallen heroes of the Korean War. It is also striking in its powerful artistic design, the centerpiece being an actual battle ground scene on which a group of nineteen larger-than-life– sized soldiers are depicted in stainless steel and who are in a stance of a perpetual advancing patrol, the realistic features on the faces of the men all showing their fear as well as courage. Complementing the scene and similar to the Vietnam wall is another long wall but instead of the roster of etched names, here the actual faces of the soldiers are etched beautifully but painfully into the granite, nameless they look out at you like ghosts. This too was powerfully moving.

The Roosevelt Memorial isn't tragic like the others because it tells the story of this great man's courage and contribution in WWII joining with the Brits in the battle to beat Hitler and fascism, and his own exceptional courage and personal bravery battling for decades his infirmity from polio, leaving his legs paralyzed, requiring crutches and the ever-present need for physical support. As you journey through these special spaces it feels more like a respectful, historic exhibit—very meaningful and inspiring. But the tragedy of war does become sadly and strongly evident as the telling of its story and those of previous battles in earlier times unfolds.

I was ready now for the posh and buzzy Washington neighborhood known as Georgetown, which was within walking distance of down-town being approximately only two miles away from all the famous buildings, monuments, and other well- known sites. The busy main street running east and west coming out of Washington was simply called M street, and the other main north and south road was called Wisconsin and where they converged was the hub of downtown Georgetown. Both were continually filled with as many yellow taxis as general traffic coming to and from downtown Washington. Georgetown was hopping twenty-four hours a day with restaurants, bookshops, clubs, and very tempting and desirable shopping and was a lovely area to walk and explore, at any time of the day and night. Walking south the streets start to slope as they wind down to the lazy Potomac River, which offered boat trips and lots of fun bars and eating places to enjoy, a great place to people watch, while sitting at a sunny café sipping a frothy coffee—before the Starbucks mania began. Revived, I would turn back up the hill heading north, randomly exploring parts of Georgetown that were off the beaten track, and zigzag up and down charming cobble stone streets, discovering large, lovely old homes sitting next to small- and medium-size row homes on the same street and all of them with charming blooming gardens, whatever the season. There were also many small public parks lovingly tended with seasoned wooden benches for rest and contemplation. I would often take visitors who were lovers of fine gardens to my favorite place, the impressive Dumbarton Oaks museum and gardens—an exceptional surprise—an ultra-traditional Georgian façade concealing a priceless treasure trove of pre-Columbian, Roman, and Byzantine artifacts and administered by Harvard University, which was deeded the house, gardens, and collection in 1940. Set on ten acres of formal gardens, considered among America's best, we would stroll downhill as the gardens unfolded on a series of broad terraces with trees shading us as we walked among the colorful blooms that changed with the season. And on a warm summer night, you could often catch a concert performed on the terraces, under the stars—idyllic!

On an energetic excursion I could make it all the way up to the Washington National Cathedral built on the commanding site on Mount Saint Alban, where on a clear day you could see all the way across the city to Capitol Hill, which was no coincidence, the site for the cathedral having been deliberately chosen as a reminder to the occupants of Capitol Hill that the Almighty and the cathedral's bishops had the politicians in their sights and in their prayers day and night. The Protestant Episcopal Cathedral Church of Saint Peter and Saint Paul was the sixth largest cathedral in the world and an awe-inspiring creation, which in Pierre L'Enfant's "Plan of the Federal City" (which set aside land, though not this bit) for a "great church for national purposes," it had clearly been a long-awaited project. Finally, a charter to build the cathedral was passed in January 1893 and the foundation stone was laid in the presence of President Theodore Roosevelt and a crowd of more than twenty thousand in September 1907. The building of the great cathedral ended eighty-three years later when the last finial was set in place in 1990, but still the decorative work would continue for many more years. Congress designated the Washington National Cathedral as the National House of Prayer, and during World War II monthly services were held there "on behalf of a united people in time of emergency." Before and since, the building has hosted other major national events, both religious and secular, including lots of funerals for very important women and men, all of whom had made a contribution which drew the attention and interest of the American people. The

Photo courtesy Linda Glisson

Washington National Cathedral drew my attention too, and I fell in love with it immediately, and when I discovered it also had a reputation for good music and a fine choral tradition, I decided that this splendid space would be my next singing venue, just as soon as I was a settled, permanent resident of the city, a Washingtonian! I knew little about this national treasure but I was naturally struck and delighted by how English the cathedral's Neo Gothic design was. George Frederick Bodley, Britain's leading Anglican Church architect, had been appointed by the first Episcopal bishop of the Washington Diocese in the 1800s and given the enviable job as the head architect of the enormous project. It's final design shows a mix of influences from the various Gothic architectural styles of the Middle Ages, identifiable in its pointed arches, flying buttresses, a variety of ceiling vaulting, stained -glass windows, and carved decorations in stone, including gargoyles, and by its three similar towers, two on the west front and one surmounting the crossing. Intricate woodcarving, wall-sized murals, mosaics, and monumental cast bronze gates can also be found.

Most of the decorative elements have Christian symbolism, in reference to the church's Episcopalian roots, but the cathedral is also filled with memorials to persons or events of national significance: statues of Washington and Lincoln, state seals embedded in the marble floor of the narthex, state flags that hang along the nave, stained glass commemorating events like the Lewis and Clark expedition and the raising of the American flag at Iwo Jima. The cathedral's interior consists of a long, narrow rectangular mass formed by a nine-bay nave with wide side aisles and a five bay chancel, intersected by a six bay transept. The pulpit was carved out of stones from the great English religious sights of Glastonbury Abbey and Canterbury Cathedral. The abbey also provided the stone for the bishop's formal seat, the cathedra. The high alter was called the Jerusalem Alter and made from stones quarried at Solomon's Quarry near Jerusalem, which is reputedly where the stones for Solomon's Temple were also quarried. There are many other works of art including over two hundred stained glass windows, the most famous of which may be the Space Window, honoring man's landing on the Moon, which includes a fragment of lunar rock at its center. I signed up to take tours to learn as much as I could about the history of the new cathedral.

One of the most poignant stories told by the tour guide was about the many Italian stone masons whose skill was unsurpassed and who had been brought over from Italy and employed to work on the cathedral. One of the workers approached the bishop with the news that his wife was very ill and asked permission for a plot of ground for her burial when the time came. With great regret the bishop was forced to decline the request simply because there was no land available—not for any burials. The cathedral had very little land around it, only enough for a small garden. A few months later the bishop saw the man again happily whistling as he worked and inquired about his wife. Sadly, she had died, but the mason seemed quite happy—"You seem content, my son," the Bishop said. "Did you find a good place to bury your wife?" "Oh yes, Your Holiness," the man replied. "I am happy that she will always be very close beside me. I mixed her ashes in my cement so that she could be a part of this great cathedral and smile down on us at all time." Concealing a furrowed brow the bishop apparently blessed the man and as he hurried away he murmured that he wouldn't say a word about this to a living soul.

Although I flirted frequently with agnosticism, believing that more care concerning the human condition could and should be done here on earth than could be expected to be done in the heavens, I was still drawn to the spiritual music of the great composers and was conscious of a spirituality felt in those special places of the great outdoors as much as in old churches and even new cathedrals. I had a soft spot for the Humanity of Man, even though both Man and God frequently disappointed me. I loved the cathedral and was happy to have such a splendid building so close to where I now lived, but it made me think again and feel homesick for the hundreds of ancient churches and cathedrals many dating back more than a thousand years that are dotted all over the English countryside, and can be found in her cities, towns, and villages, large and small. I was reminded of one particular and favorite cathedral, begun in the year 1220, the main body being "a medieval mountain of carved stone." The high vaulting of the roofs interior or clearstory in the upper area of the nave are in the early English Gothic style, but perhaps its most loved and recognized feature is the 404-foot spire of vertical supremacy, a slim elegant spire whose serenity and simplicity can be seen for many miles around.

Salisbury Cathedral was always an inspiration and has been

painted by many of the great artists, Constable, Turner, and Whistler among them. It sits quietly in a meadow on the Salisbury Plain in the magical county of Wiltshire, close to the small market town of Salisbury in the southwest of England, and it has sat there for nearly eight hundred years. This county has enormous 'Q' (quaint) factor. I thought that one interesting comparison is the length of time the new cathedral in Washington took to build compared to the old cathedral in Salisbury. It took eighty-three years to build the Washington National Cathedral, but all those centuries ago, it took only thirty-eight years and three hundred men to build the Salisbury Cathedral, and that includes the tallest spire in the land, and also the tallest medieval building in the world. Salisbury Cathedral is a wonderful example and considered a thoroughbred of early English Gothic. Equally impressive is the fact that after all these centuries, it hasn't fallen down, and sitting as it does on a gravel river bed with foundations that are only four feet deep makes it even more amazing! Clearly some divine intervention continues to be at play watching over this heavenly inspired, great creation of man! Before I drag myself away from happy memories of Wiltshire, I should mention that the county also has a few other well-known and amazing sites that I love and I would be remiss not to add them to its fascinating list. They include the intriguing and amazing Stonehenge, built around 3,000–2,500 BC, also the mysterious White Horses—thirteen of them—built into the white chalk hills, a fascinating feature and accomplishment found across Wiltshire. These impressive carvings were worked by the ancients into the chalk hills and they wanted their impressive hard labor to be admired for miles around, so they deliberately made the carvings both very large and very deep thereby revealing the whiteness of the chalk underneath. There is also Old Sarum, an ancient Iron Age hill fort that rises to 1,200 feet and where there is evidence of Roman, Saxon, and Norman settlements. It has to be something very special to be more impressive than Stonehenge, but arguably the Avebury Stone Circle is considered more impressive because it is approximately the same age but it is also the largest stone circle in the world, almost entirely encompassing the tranquil village of Avebury, in England's pretty county of Wiltshire.

I have always liked to look forward and backward in time, making comparisons, looking for the links that connect us to the old and ancient world regardless of how many years, decades, or centuries that connection may be. It is the continuation of the thread that's important, and we can grasp hold of that thread because it is easy to see and it is all around us. For me these two cathedrals make for a good comparison, joined as they are by the same spiritual idea and the need for a physical place to congregate and express that idea. The space and design of the cathedral in Washington was developed from a style of building originally seen eight hundred years ago, and it came from a small village, which was three thousand miles away. The journey made by those ideas was both arduous and seemingly impossible, a struggle fraught with every kind of difficulty and obstruction, including the danger of the usual suspects of war, plague, and ignorance that came out and blocked them nearly every step of the way. But determination and eternal courage gradually beat down those obstacles until that journey of time and distance was overcome, and this new magnet, another great mountain of stone, a great cathedral, stood completed before us, a worthy beacon and a comfort to a beautiful and important capital city and a nation. I never forget that we "stand on the shoulders of giants." In so many ways we are what they made us. Of course, even the design of the great cathedral of Salisbury was not the first of its kind. We can look back even farther in time and be humbled by the great early cathedral builders from France and even earlier to the ancient Greeks themselves whose contribution in applying early mathematical ideas still informs us today. Mankind has toiled for thousands of years in their struggle to make sure that a great heavy pile of stones would not always fall to the ground but would continue to stand, becoming stronger and gradually taller as they built higher toward the sky and to the glory of their God. Faith, human ingenuity, determination, mathematics, courage, and great endeavor all contributed and were essential in assuring that a great pile of stones would not always fall but would continue to stand and hopefully stay safely in place for all time.

Each of us remolds and reshapes the clay we are given so it too will echo with our own identity and become the contribution we make, the one that reflects and fits with our own short time. The distance hadn't changed, and here was I, still the same three thousand miles away from my real homeland, as witness to the respect and love of an ancient idea. I was standing in front of the Cathedral Church of Saint Peter and Saint Paul, the Washington National Cathedral, which was an eight hundred year updated version of the great twelfth century cathedral still sitting in a river bed in a meadow in Salisbury, Wiltshire, England. But it was here in Washington's cathedral that I would bring my voice and continue to sing.

CHAPTER 5
PART TWO

The Official Life

After the normal, but lengthy wait, Richard was formally called to serve by going through a modern ritual in a court of law where he would be officially confirmed as the United States Assistant Secretary of Commerce. The senate committee was officiated over by a jolly chap, Senator Fritz Hollings, from South Carolina. I was even asked to sing for the assembled company during the celebratory procedures when my own resume with my BSO experiences were revealed, but I humbly declined, it was after all, Richard's big day and I still didn't have all the words of the National Anthem completely secure and at my command. Richard had a large crowd of well-wishers, personal friends and relatives, IRI friends and staff along with Richard's own staff from the Commerce Department at his swearing-in ceremony. There followed an enjoyable celebratory luncheon at one of the Hill restaurants, where the wait staff seemed somewhat unimpressed at yet another swearing-in ceremony.

Richard had already been working in the position at the Commerce Department for nearly six months before he was officially sworn in. Finally in March of 1993, it was official. There is often a prolonged period before the position becomes official and this is not unusual, but he had quickly won over his staff and already had many projects up and running. It was a wonderful fit for him and I watched him as he visibly soared in the role, understanding all aspects and requirements of the issues and agenda. Richard did the job with his keen, broad intelligence and a deep knowledge of the issues. He also added a mix of English humor and with his general aplomb he became respected and admired by all who came in contact with him.

We had moved into a dreamy, spacious, three-story townhouse in Georgetown by now. It was beautifully designed and sat in a quiet area, which was set high up on an attractive hilly landscape and also included facilities, meaning a lovely open air pool area and lighted tennis courts, and it was only a five-minute walk from Georgetown. It was a gated community with a happy but official guard at the gate-house who remembered our names and gave us a cheery chat and a wave every day. We soon met and became very good friends with a number of our neighbors, who were on the staff from a number of the surrounding embassies and I enjoyed the cosmopolitan atmosphere and social occasions that those friendships created.

Few of us have the opportunities that we were now exposed to on a daily basis. It was all good and it was exciting and stimulating and, of course, I realized that it was also an honor to experience this life, unusual as it was in its own way. Since our arrival in Washington we had started receiving numerous invitations to attend internal functions at other US Departments, but also formal invitations to foreign embassy functions. It was an important part of the job. On average we would attend two functions a night; embassy-hopping I called it. At the weekend we often hunkered down and took the phone of the hook so we could rest and replenish our energies for the following weeks' round of official social attendance.

Diplomacy is the all-important tool, and during the time, Richard held the position at the Commerce Department he was invited to official diplomatic meetings and conferences in many different countries on the subject of science and technology in the national interest, and these often came at the invitation of those representatives and contacts he had met at their Washington embassies. These meeting were mutually beneficial on both sides, enabling them to continue to embrace more broadly those good ideas they shared, while mitigating any possible concerns, all the while strengthening the mutual collaboration of both sides. While the collaboration benefitted both countries, it was also genuine diplomacy at work. With the flag of each nation fluttering from a prominent point outside the embassy, on entering you felt as though you had stepped inside that particular country and were about to experience a generous slice of the country's culture. As with all the embassies, their costume, customs, food, and even music is specifically meant to represent that country, even the internal décor reflects this down to the last detail. They are a home away from home for the ambassador and his or her staff. By the same token, when we stepped over their threshold and entered one of these embassies, we did so as America's true and trusted representatives. It was a fascinating and gracious experience, and an honor to exercise.

We naturally had a few favorites and were delighted by invitations from certain embassies where there was an immediate camaraderie. The Canadian embassy always greeted us with the required formality coupled with a back-slapping pleasure and genuine enthusiasm that comes with the comfortable connection of the like-minded and those of shared humor. Their spread was always an amazing and scrumptious array of the freshest "fruits of the sea" from beautiful Nova Scotia. We also looked forward to the genuine warmth and hospitality of both the Czech and

Hungarian embassies, which were easy, relaxed, and polite, and we thoroughly enjoyed their tasty, hearty food offering, more delicious pork dishes than I knew existed.

The Japanese delegation was housed in a spacious, elegant, turn-of-the-century house situated along what is known as Embassy Row, an area including the lovely long avenues of Massachusetts and Wisconsin. Many of the 175 foreign embassies that are located in the nation's capital are historic mansions and are clustered close to one another, on or near the Embassy Row area. The Japanese Embassy had some exquisite features. Delicate fine- brush artwork decorated the walls and small sculptures sat on perfect surfaces, while music tinkled softly in the background, providing a perfect balance of Asian sophistication. Each nation did this, proudly showing off their own particular heritage, evoking their own traditional style. The Japanese food was a gasp for the taste buds, that's if you like sushi, which happily we did, and after engaging in polite conversation, we would head over to a visual feast, not just for the eyes but for the palate.

We enjoyed the short walk to the French Embassy from our house. We have visited France on many occasions, it being so close and easy to travel there from England, one could even say it was a swimmable distance for some. So we had always had a soft spot for France, the French people and their customs, and in keeping with other embassies who offered a proud open window into their country's national character, so did the French. Compared with most of the other embassies, it was decidedly understated; there was nothing ostentatious about it. The embassy was like a French home away from home and everyone felt quietly comfortable in the space they had created for themselves and the embassy staff was also imbued with the same qualities of congenial confidence. To me, its atmosphere felt the way the music of Debussy sounds. The usual overwhelming spread of food found at other embassies was absent here, instead delicious morsels of savory and sweet foods were displayed on elegant tables and offered from small silver trays so you could always keep hold of your glass of the very best French wine while using the other fingers to sample the exquisite hors d'oeuvres being offered. The walls displayed a sampling for the eyes of an understated arrangement of French art while in the background the strains of Ravel or Debussy swept softly over you. It was divine. We also received fairly frequent invitations from the French Embassy to attend one of their evening musical soirees, a trio or quartet or a simple piano recital. For me this was the height of delight.

A large, modern, and rather imposing structure sat high on top of a steep hill which gave a commanding view of a cascade of lovely terraces that made up the garden. This was the German Embassy where we were also frequently invited and they really loved to put on a good show. In warm weather they utilized the colorful garden terraces where guests could sit at tables under small trees decorated with little lights, while fluttering tablecloths played with the breeze. A boisterous, fun-loving crowd of guests and hosts alike put aside the problems of the world while they quenched summer thirsts from the excellent cold beer brought in from the finest German breweries, which flowed from the authentic barrels conveniently situated among the crowd. The ambassador and his staff were very congenial and genuinely wanted everyone to enjoy themselves at these garden parties, going out of their way to make sure they did. The perfect complement to the beer was German cabbage and potato salad, which went well with the fifty varieties of German sausage and black bread on offer to soak up the beer. The food did go perfectly with the beer and amid the loud laughter the guests showed their approval by always enjoying themselves– a perfect fit.

The Australian Embassy was great, absolutely no formal protocol here. Everyone was very laid back and they all had an infectious sense of humor, and on every occasion, they welcomed us as old friends. Richard was even invited to watch some international rugby matches in a very informal, male-only, beer-drinking setting. They wanted all the guests to relax the way they did, no stuffed shirts were allowed, which in a decidedly stuffed shirt town, was quite refreshing. " G'day to ya, have a beer mate and I'll throw a shrimp on the barbe" definitely summed it up. Certainly we laughed more with the Aussies than with any of the other groups—laughter and good will maketh diplomacy in its own way. Not surprisingly and in many splendid ways, these happy, open Australians were a very refreshing crowd, who managed to be deeply informed on all the issues, being both naturally welcoming and hospitable at the same time, while standing on no ceremony at all.

The Korean Embassy was completely different. Sitting outside the city in a suburban setting, the embassy had been constructed from an original plan to look like a typical ancient Korean palace, and from the moment you crossed the threshold, your senses were challenged in a variety of ways. It was both an exciting and compelling place to visit and perhaps more than any other embassy I really felt transported to a strange and very different culture. Our gracious hosts greeted us clad in traditional Korean dress, and all the embassy staff wore the same exquisite long silk gowns as they served platters of very unusual food, which it was simply easier and more polite to eat rather than to question what it was. The inner courtyard was set with small decorative tables also holding small plates and bowls of strange food. In the corners of the courtyard were huge stone jars or "vats" standing about six feet tall where traditionally "decomposing cabbage" ferments away and keeps Korean families fed throughout good times and bad. It is called Kimchi, a national comfort dish, something like fish and chips or hot dogs I suppose. If you didn't know what it was it could be quite tasty; it resembled what I imagined sloppy coleslaw might taste like—coleslaw that might have passed its sell-by date!

Moving right along, but hopefully not immediately following the Korean fare, was the Chinese Embassy. The Washington home of the Chinese delegation was a vast mansion strategically placed in a position of prominence on Wisconsin Avenue, part of the Embassy Row. Everything about it seemed large and very impressive. The walls of the embassy were filled with very unusual pieces of Chinese art. The art was exceptional and worked well with the many other artifacts on display in this unusual venue. Large ceramic works of art complemented the exquisite rugs and carpeting, which were displayed both on the walls and the floors giving the mansion its warmth. The hospitality was friendly and formal and the food offered for the guests was set out on a huge long table. Many of the dishes were recognizable but there were also some delicious surprises if you could sort them out, and the fortune cookies were always in plentiful supply.

Bringing up the rear of this slog-fest embassy tour has to be the British Embassy strategically situated on Massachusetts Avenue. It is the first house on the elegant and famous Embassy Row and you can't miss it because of its huge, easily recognizable oversized bronze sculptured rendition of Sir Winston Churchill himself, with his faithful cigar and scrutinizing glare, daring the bravest among us not to even think of setting foot on the embassy's English soil without a very visible invitation waving in their hand. Perhaps a comforting figure for those of us old enough to remember World War II, showing the steely, steadfast grit, and determination of the English at war, especially against those Germans up there on their terraced, hilly vantage point, eating their sausages. I had already met a few of the English embassy wives at luncheons and small tea parties and exchanged the required formal pleasantries. I loved the embassy's elegant architecture, which was designed and built by the notable English architect Sir Edward Lutyens, 1869–1944, who was often described (by the

Brits) as the greatest architect of his age. There are examples of his work all over England and in many other countries, mostly of the former British colonies. For the British Embassy, he chose an understated and revived version of the 1702–1714 Queen Anne style, an updated design that was popular in the last quarter of the nineteenth and early twentieth centuries. It was moderately ornate, using red-brick walls contrasting with pale stone details. Luyten also made beautiful furniture and was known for his perfectly complimentary interior decor which, of course, balanced so well with the outside structure of slightly understated grandeur.

As a young, faithful, history- loving English citizen of my younger days, I was always touring around looking in awe at the nations' long history revealed in its architecture and in the bricks and mortar that held together those great stately homes, many of which had now become not so stately but wards of the state because they had become too drafty, uncomfortable, and expensive for the aristos to keep them up on their own, so they were now run by the National Trust and open to the public for a fee, even though they were already helping to foot the bill for some of the upkeep in their taxes. The English didn't mind because they are not just curious about their long, entertaining history; they are sometimes downright nosey, trying to keep all the dates correct (hoping to be asked) and they enjoy muttering and tut-tutting quietly while politely poking around to see what splendors had been captured and amassed after this battle or that, or where the dastedly deed of murder had occurred and to whom and by whom (can we still see the blood), but better still what devious liaisons or juicy hanky-panky had happened to whom and by whom and in which bed and in what room. Since we can assume that many of these very human activities had occurred on a frequent basis, once a month, week or in case of the hanky-panky, once a day for hundreds of years, the numbers are mind boggling. The visitors loved it all and wandered through every dusty room, which told one eerie story after another, imagining themselves sleeping in the old four-poster bed or sitting around in an oversize winged chair, staring nostalgically at the walk-in fireplace, trying to warm themselves on the fire's long dead embers. This intimate exposure to history is why the Brits are always writing and winning awards for their television period series, which they, and I, cannot get enough of. And of course, as you might guess, among the most popular stately homes are those built in the Queen Ann style, perhaps because they all looked so pretty and so perfect and were always very inviting even though much that was not so pretty or perfect had been going on for hundreds of years behind those closed doors!

But it was all understated elegance and the finest of English manners with the Brits at the British Embassy and part of me loved it and pined to be in its presence. But there was another all too familiar, giveaway characteristic that was present and was reminiscent of growing up in England, and that was the not-so-good, good old class system and it was immediately recognizable and on display just as the first, overly exaggerated vowel dropped from a smiling, welcoming mouth. That language of the privileged upper classes was in place certainly before Charles Dickens's time, because he uses those extreme contrasts in the behavior and dialogue to color the language of his characters.

It first became organized in the so-called public schools, which suggests they were open to the public at large, which could not have been further from the truth. They were in in fact very private schools where rich young boys were sent to become well groomed in everything. This grooming included speech, and the correct, or some say distorted, pronunciation of the vowel that went with it. Being classically educated also meant they were being groomed for the officer class in the military or in politics or rarified businesses, where it was considered essential to give orders in an authoritatively "upper class" way if you wanted to be obeyed. It naturally permeated through all sections of the moneyed echelons, which is why in BBC renditions of period pieces, the better educated upstairs people always speak in a more affected and authoritative way than those who are downstairs. It is deliberate. The privileged education that taught this hybrid form of speech created a distorted, language of exaggerated vowels, which produced the upper-class accent and it had as its purpose a way to separate the rich from the rest—and it was successful. While it is generally agreed that it was deliberately designed to create a powerful class distinction, from the royals themselves down, it did in the process also distort the English language itself. One expects and enjoys the regional differences in vowel sounds and word pronunciation, and they have all grown naturally, as if out of the soil, and they began developing from many various influences more than a thousand years ago. Despite this small, amusing irk, we thoroughly enjoyed and did make friends among the embassy Brits, but sometimes I felt a distance—perhaps we didn't have the right accent and were gently regarded as deserters, never unkindly or deliberately, but we had, after all, made a choice to become citizens of a foreign land, and even worse, America was the battle the Brits lost!

So I gratefully welcomed and received a crash course in foreign diplomacy simply by being in attendance, I learned on the job. But the subject of diplomatic civility, both national and international, was an art form, honed over centuries and found in countries all over the world. As a result there was an expected and cultivated mode of polite, even gracious behavior, required at all times when dealing with a representative of any foreign embassy whether as your own guest or as a guest invited to an embassy. This was especially true as an invited guest at a foreign embassy. The real estate on which any embassy stands becomes the sovereign space of that country. The embassy staff all looked, dressed, and behaved courteously at all times, enacting their country's customs proudly and comfortably as if they were physically residing in their own country and you had been their invited guest. It was a privilege to be asked to participate in this age-old system of acknowledgment and respect, where much was expected and much was received.

The best way to balance the heady whirlwind that was now my life was to have some family around, and in the summer of 1994, with his shiny new history degree in hand, Andrew joined us in Washington and took up residence with us in the conveniently situated ground floor flat where he had a comfortable sitting area, which converted to a sleeping area and with an adjoining private bathroom. Andrew was a city person and he came and went as he pleased, exploring on foot every area of this, his new city. In his first year in DC, he made his mother very happy when he immediately got a job with US Airways in their marketing department where one of their perks extended down to immediate family members, which offered stand-by free flights within the United States. I now felt settled and secure and happy in my new home and new city. My daughter Beth was very well and happy working on her post-doctorate in the UK. She also had a serious, new, Scottish-born boyfriend, an environmental geologist who spent long periods of time working on an oil rig in the North Sea. After a year Andrew decided that the rat-race in corporate America was not a good fit for him and found he could make a better contribution in the non-profit world of professional fund raising where he could make a real difference. He also found himself an apartment and began meeting new, like-minded people, making good friends and enjoying his life in the new city. Richard was enjoying his position enormously and was increasingly well regarded and respected for all the contributions he was making on behalf of the country at the Commerce Department. I was very happy in my new home, which lent itself to easy and enjoyable entertaining, and I was also comfortable in my various new roles, understanding and enjoying what was expected of me as the wife of an assistant secretary. So all was well and I knew it was time to go back to the cathedral and enjoy what I loved most, the opportunity to sing again. I auditioned to join the Cathedral Choral Society and happily looked forward to the joy that came in filling that glorious space with the sound of voices singing glorious music.

J. Reilly Lewis was the fine music director of the chorus with high expectations from each member of the group. Reilly was also recognized internationally as a conductor and keyboard artist as well as a specialist in baroque music, especially the music of J. S. Bach. The Cathedral Choral Society is the resident symphonic chorus of the cathedral and provided an important role in the cathedral's outreach activities. But this was not the Tanglewood Festival Chorus, which had fewer singers, but where each voice had huge volume and special agility, which gave it its individuality and a soloist quality, which was what John Oliver was looking for in his auditions. Also much more was demanded of us being the resident chorus of the Boston Symphony—there was such a thing as status. We had a high public profile and much was expected of us individually in terms of the number of different works we studied privately and performed annually at numerous public appearances, memorization was a constant requirement, recordings were frequent, and international travel was also involved. It was a way of life.

The Cathedral Choral Society was founded in 1941 by Paul Callaway, who served as its music director until 1984. Since then J. Reilly Lewis has conducted the society in many specially commissioned works as well as the musical masterpieces of the great composers and to plain-song and contemporary works. Their mission was to promote and perform the highest quality choral music for the nation's capital, and for national and international audiences. This was a committed larger group of 250 women and men who were also good singers and they all respected the very high expectations demanded of them and were devoted to Reilly and to the challenging choices he made for the group to sing. The rehearsals were weekly with the usual double rehearsals with orchestra just before a concert, and there were far fewer concerts, only four a year, which fitted well with the other demands in my life. Usually we had a full orchestra to accompany us unless the score was written a cappella and every cathedral concert was a sell-out with more than two thousand people in the audience. All the concerts we performed were recorded live, and many were released for general sale. At that time in my life it was a comfortable fit for me, not as competitive as TFC where we sometimes thought and behaved as though we were all prima donnas and in an easy, friendly way tended to compete with one another. But here, for me at this time, I was not only happy to have my voice join with other singers, it was also the pleasure and a feeling close to humility that I experienced when rehearsing and performing in this lovely cathedral. It had more of a spiritual feeling than a religious certainty in it for me, and there was something of a yearning and also of a childhood remembrance and of making those strong connections to the past. It was a special place because it reminded me of Salisbury and all the other great cathedrals I knew in England and their long association with music and with singing voices that produced a strong emotion in me and it caught me every time. I think it had a lot to do with the thread and the continuity I referred to earlier. It was a thrill to open and walk through the huge, heavy doors at the main entrance where immediately you were in a different world. An almost imperceptible welcoming smell of wood and stone and dust and polish and incense greeted you. I would take my time, slowly making my way down the long, softly lit nave passed the stained glass windows, murals, mosaics, and monumental cast bronze, my eye catching new small treasures each time, until I reached the rehearsal space just below the choir stalls where I became one of the early group of singers who were quietly greeting one another. Whatever the day or the week had brought in terms of happy surprises or challenges, they all quickly faded away as the great space enveloped me in an embrace, offering a stillness, anticipation, a reverence, and "the peace that passeth all understanding."

※

On April 3, 1996, that peace seemed suddenly to have evaporated. The weather was atrocious in and around the ancient walled city of Dubrovnik with intermittent heavy and driving rain for many hours, and although it had momentarily halted, the dark clouds still hung low over the nearby mountains. As Lenadra Gluhan was drinking coffee in her kitchen she heard an airplane roar overhead. This was not unusual, as an assistant air traffic controller at the nearby Dubrovnik airport, she was used to the sounds of aircraft. Hearing jets scream over her dwelling was a normal feature of her life. But it was not the sound of the jet that caught her attention; it was its direction. What it meant to her trained ear was that whoever was flying that plane was dangerously off course.

Secretary of State Ron Brown had put together an important trade mission and delegation to the Balkans, which would be extremely successful for the United States and also for the small countries in the region still reeling in recovery from the horrible Balkans war. Everyone involved was satisfied with the outcome of the trip and his trade mission had achieved good results for all concerned and was almost complete. Ron Brown was eager to be home in time for Easter, but at the last minute, an idea came up which was sanctioned by Peter Galbraith, the American ambassador in Zagreb, that the group make a stop in Dubrovnik for a photo op. The beautiful, twelve-hundred-year-old walled city, an ancient port on the Adriatic had been one of the region's prime tourist destinations before it was seriously damaged by the Serbian artillery during the vicious war between Serbia and Croatia. A photograph of the charismatic American Secretary of Commerce strolling through its quaint cobbled streets could turn business around for the city by sending a positive message to the world that Dubrovnik was back in business and could be relied upon in all ways as a tourist destination. Also a photo of the handsome Secretary Ronald Brown would be considered a great honor and a generous favor, and staying friends with those newly made friends could also bring benefits to the United States in the future. Life has a way of turning on a dime, and tragically, on its way to Dubrovnik for the photo op, the plane flew off course into the storm and careened through the wretched weather toward the mountain side. The eternal optimist, Ron Brown and his team probably had a few minutes to relax and savor the success of the trade mission, of the good partners they had made, and the welcome optimism they had brought to this interesting but struggling part of Europe, now with one last short stop they were looking forward to being back home with family and with friends where they would be celebrating the upcoming Easter weekend together, in the nation's capital where the spring and the cherry trees were offering up their magic, safely on the ground.

Rumblings of disbelief had begun to be heard in Washington early the following morning, but very few facts had been confirmed. What most people knew was that the plane was missing, but few details followed that grim fact. As the minutes of agony ticked on for the general staff and for those close colleagues in Ron Brown's inner circle, everyone was struggling to hold onto positive thoughts of hope, but gradually the mood darkened as denial and disbelief fought against truth coming from the repetitive sketchy facts being broadcast from all the news sources. A tidal wave of non-stop phone calls began coming into the secretary's office and all other offices from the many family members who had loved ones on board all hoping that members of the staff in Washington would be able to give words of reassurance about the fate of all the other members of the trade mission on that plane. There was no good news to be had. For the pilots seeing the craggy mountain side suddenly emerge from the fog, it was too late to avert the inevitable and travelling at 138 knots, the 737 plane slammed into the mountain side. The sound of the jet crashing and lives ending were lost amid the desolate terrain and the thunderclaps of the dreary Dalmatian storm. Finally the news reports told everyone that the fatal crash had snuffed out the life of Ronald Brown along with the lives of the thirty-four other passengers and crew.

Once more the National Cathedral offered itself as a place to grieve and a place to receive the consolation that we all desperately needed. We were given the necessary tickets to attend the memorial service and all of the 2,800 seats in the cathedral were taken. I am not sure how much consolation we each received, mostly we were simply given permission to weep openly. There were many notable speakers who paid homage to Ron Brown, but his long-time friend and admirer, the showman, President Bill Clinton, did the most admirable job talking about his friend Ron, even telling stories that allowed us to offer up a small smile, but generally the sorrow hung heavy on our shoulders. The shock waves lasted many weeks and they invaded every corner of the Commerce Department and were expressed by the lowliest government employee up the chain of command to the department heads. Every newspaper carried on-going coverage and an investigation went on for months addressing the notion that there was a conspiracy theory and a cover-up in play, and theories sprouted daily leading to a slew of hastily written books by ambitious writers on the "real" cause of his death. No conspiracy was ever proved.

A new secretary was needed and quickly; the nation's business needs to be seamless. And so slowly, one day at a time, the Commerce Department resumed the nation's business. After a few months a new secretary from Chicago was sworn in to head the Department of Commerce, and he brought with him his own staff, which was usual in any transition; there is always a changing of the guard. But it was still the president in the White House who set the agenda that had to be followed. Staff changes are not at all unusual in politics. There are frequently moves among staffers, but on this occasion coming on top of the situation caused by Ron Brown's untimely and tragic death, the atmosphere at the department was one of deep sadness and disbelief and uncertainty.

Some people were already moving on, or thinking about it including Dr. Ann Harris. Richard remained in place for a few months but there are always changes to be made in any major reshuffling plan, and he was among many who found themselves in that position. What to do? Move on seems to have always been the answer. Some months were spent pondering other options in Washington, which was where we both preferred to be, but there would be nothing as attractive as the four and a half years spent in his role as assistant secretary for Technology Policy. It was a shock and a disappointment not only for Richard but also for me and it began inevitably to look like another move was on the horizon.

Amid this upheaval a string of events happened quickly and closely together, one on the heels of another leaving little time in between to reflect on each of them. My dog Josephine, a loving and trusty companion for twelve years who knew Washington almost as well as I did, died suddenly. At the same time I received the very happy, welcome news that a wedding was being arranged by my daughter in England, but alas, little involvement was required from me. I was, of course, delighted for her but also saddened by the fact that distance would prevent me from playing the traditional role of mother of the bride, but I did what I could from three thousand miles away to offer some thoughts and suggestions for Beth in her wedding plans for the special day. But the big decisions had been made and other plans had already been worked out, and everything was under control so there was very little for the mother of the bride to do and my input seemed unnecessary. Both Beth and Antony knew exactly what they wanted and wearing flowers in her hair and a beautiful long rich, blue velvet gown which coordinated perfectly with the color in Antony's full traditional Highland attire of kilt and sporran, they looked a lovely and very happy couple on the day. A classical violin quartet serenaded the guests as they arrived for the perfect reception, which was held in a small but charming country hotel where they served delicious food. We took over the place and dancing along with general jollity continued after the meal, and I was the very, very happy and proud mother of the bride. Although I still felt I had missed out on the excitement of helping to plan my only daughters' wedding, I also realized that when you have raised a very independent child who has lived away from home and in another country for fourteen years, it isn't surprising that she would know exactly what she wanted, and from then on, I knew I would always be able to trust her judgment even if it meant being kept at a distance.

After much floor pacing and deep conversations over many months with friends and colleagues, Richard finally decided on a job offer. It was settled, and in 1998 he would become a Visiting Professor for Entrepreneurship at the Wharton School of the University of Pennsylvania, and Director of the Wharton Program in Technological Innovation, all of which was a very good fit for him. So it was back to Philadelphia! I was in a sea of emotional turmoil. Farewell parties and dinners are not as much fun as the welcoming ones and I had to force myself to many of them feeling that great wrench again, like a dragging undertow, underway inside me.

Housing prices had fallen and it was a very bad time to sell but we were very lucky to find a judge from California and his wife who loved our house. He had just been called to serve in the administration and wanted to rent our town house in Georgetown for two years by which time we hoped the housing market would have recovered, and we would be able to sell our house. The thought of leaving my lovely house and the interesting and rarefied life we had lived for four and a half years to move back to Philadelphia for the second time in my life did not fill me with great joy. I knew it would be a very hard adjustment, so I decided to hold on to my roots in Washington for one more year and decided to continue to sing with the Cathedral Chorus, which would mean driving three hours there and back, once every week from Philadelphia and staying overnight with willing, supportive friends and also with my own complicit son. But by this time Beth had also been offered a post doc research position at the University of Pennsylvania at the medical school and would also be living in the city of Brotherly Love with her new husband Antony, and this fact complicated my decision even more. I was, of course, delighted that we could have a family reunion and that we would all be in the same city, but I had decided that I would continue to have my own, different agenda in Washington for a while.

There were many complicated reasons I chose to do this—one of the main reasons was a need for my own independence. It meant I was not yet committed to this new move and it gave me time to think for myself and decide what I wanted and needed to do. Although I had had many unusual and deeply satisfying experiences over the years, where I had pursued successful endeavors of my own making, I had also been a supportive and compliant wife, and in spite of the wonderful perks of the last five years, I was still a slightly reluctant immigrant and I did not feel the need of a continuous commitment to spend the rest of my life following my husband around. It was complicated, but an opportunity had presented itself and it gave me a convincing reason to stand my ground, and that allowed a feeling of having some small control over my own decisions, which was what I badly needed.

The most important reason and the one that trumped all others was the opportunity to sing under the great maestro Robert Shaw and I refused to miss that opportunity. The now ageing conductor was to conduct the cathedral chorus twice, one performance at the cathedral and the second at the Kennedy Centre. The challenging but wonderful music chosen for us to sing was Beethoven's great and moving masterpiece the *Missa-Solemnis*. It would involve me spending one night and two days a week back in DC and it seemed clear to me—I had no choice. I had to sing this masterpiece and this was one experience I would not give up.

CHAPTER SIX

Coming Full Circle

Beth and Antony were there to greet us when we arrived in Philadelphia and it was an exciting and happy reunion for all of us after so many years living in different countries separated by three thousand miles. It was also a very pleasant, but oddly unexpected turn of events in some ways, to find we were all in the same city at the same time – Andrew would come later –but all of us being together at least on the same continent was certainly an event we all welcomed and celebrated. They had a small garden apartment in an old but interesting section of the city which was conveniently within walking distance to the university where Beth now worked. While looking for our own new place to live, we stayed for a few days in a hotel on the Franklin Parkway which I thought one of the most attractive areas in Philadelphia with the colorful, fluttering flags of every nation lining both sides of the broad, tree lined avenue and with the proud prominent statement made by the Philadelphia Museum of Art which you couldn't miss - a grand Greek temple to the arts, standing on high ground and presiding at the far end as the gateway to the grand Parkway and to the first, and oldest city of America beyond. Thinking we were ready for an apartment life in the city we looked everywhere in that area and in a dozen others but nowhere could we find something we liked or that we found suitable or affordable. It was a disappointing search and it didn't help that the sweltering, humid summer heat combined with the choking carbon monoxide fumes belching out of all the cars that were slowly maneuvering their way through the narrow streets, drained all our enthusiasm for city life and I began to think we should look outside the city in a leafy suburb that might bring some breathing space and shade from the oppressive atmosphere.

I left the Philadelphia problem on hold and went back to Georgetown to finish the dismantling of our Washington life and handsome home and to organize the packing of its contents for the journey further north. I stopped to reflect that I had been through this so many times I had developed some resilience against the sad repetition of so many 'goodbyes' - but I had not entirely, - why was I in this position so many times when, in truth I had never wanted to be here at all. It was also very hot back in Georgetown but somehow the openness and spacious layout of my home, the city and the happy hills of Georgetown gave some relief. While I was sadly going from room to room dismantling my home and trying to organize our belongings into those of immediate need and those which would inevitably have to be put into storage, I received a phone call from my new son-in-law in Philadelphia with encouraging news! Antony was my hero! He had been busy on our behalf and had spotted an interesting rental ad in a local newspaper for a two bedroom apartment in an old stone house built around 1880 in the handsome, garden city suburb of Chestnut Hill. I called immediately and following a lengthy, detailed conversation with the owner I liked what I heard and took a chance, trusting my judgment, and agreed to rent the flat on the spot, sight unseen, it sounded perfect, almost!

Moving day was hell, however. A major, ferocious storm

with hours of thunder and lightning was in process, tearing tree limbs down and flooding major roads causing drivers to abandon their cars by the side of the road resulting in a dreadful upheaval for all traffic in the area - it seemed a bad omen and it was certainly an uncomfortable beginning, driving as we were on unfamiliar roads, dragging an uncooperative trailer behind us. We were greeted at the door by our new landlord and lady who gave us a quick inspection of the place. The apartment itself was workable and had enough space and charm to make me smile. The house itself was indeed a very handsome property and well kept up with beautiful gardens front and back and we had our own separate parking space and entrance which took us through the back flower garden to our front door. But the narrow, tightly curved and original, antique spiral- staircase almost caused a fight when the moving men refused to carry the piano or the couch up to the third floor. It was fair enough and they had a point, but an unexpected glitch we hadn't been prepared for and one which only a considerably large, monetary bribe and an increase in the price of the job, along with a signed agreement both to the moving company and also to the owners of the house stating our acceptance for all responsibility for any damage done to the property, would appease all parties! I held my breath and hid in the bathroom not able to watch the groaning battle that raged below as both piano and couch made their torturous way around the tight curves as the movers moaned and huffed and puffed, stopping frequently to wipe the pouring sweat away from their brow. I wailed silently, but finally Richard told me it was safe to come out of hiding - both pieces and four men had made it up to the third floor, and from somewhere I spirited up enough beers to go around and invited them to sit on the couch they had just carried up the spiral staircase and rest until their heart rate had stabilized. With a great sigh of gratitude - it's amazing what money can do - I settled down and unpacked our possessions which did not look so bad in the now dry light of day and the apartment itself felt airy with lots of windows and pleasant views in all directions and was comfortable and reasonably roomy all round - and the spiral staircase to our third floor retreat provided a daily work-out exercise for both of us for the next two years.

With the boxes unpacked the place took on a pleasant homeliness and I soon became curious about my surroundings. Knowing that the apartment was going to be just fine I immediately wanted to explore the small town and discovering it to be even better than I had hoped was a another pleasant surprise I had not expected. In fact it seemed that once I had put in the required time on most of the new addresses I had had over the years I discovered many interesting historical facts and local delights that helped settle my concerns and softened my aggravation, but the process itself was often exhausting and I was very tired of a life that required constant changes which always, it seemed to me, demanded immediate physical and emotional adjustments. But I had to admit that for a time Chestnut Hill was an ideal address for us, located in the northwestern corner of Philadelphia, the town was one of the region's most beautiful and architecturally distinguished communities. Flanked by the spectacular Wissahickon Gorge and Cresheim Valley it was home to one of the best collections of 19th and early 20th-century residential buildings in the country, with every notable architect practicing from Philadelphia and beyond for over the last 150 plus years, all represented in Chestnut Hill making it both an eclectic and very attractive and interesting environment. Consequently, it was a magnet for many other unusual ideas and the town offered useful conveniences and surprises like the three attractive, little train stations with reliable service for commuting into the city, all within walking distance. Pastorius Park was in the center of town. It was a large, leafy park where children could play and concerts were regularly performed.

THE RELUCTANT IMMIGRANT

What was the name Pastorius all about? I was intrigued and wanted to know! Reading up on Mr. Pastorius revealed many interesting facts about the early beginnings of what would become Chestnut Hill and why Germantown Avenue became such an important central thoroughfare. I discovered that Francis Daniel Pastorius was a German intellectual born in 1651, a member of a wealthy, aristocratic German family, trained in the classics and in law and although he was not a Quaker himself he was sympathetic and held many of their beliefs and was soon elected the leader of a group of thirteen Quaker families from Krefeld, Germany and founded the town of Krefeld in 1683. Pastorius negotiated directly with William Penn on behalf of the German Society who agreed on a 5,700 tract of land, the German Township, located six miles northwest of Philadelphia, and in 1686 Pastorius reported on the construction of a 'kirchlein' or 'little church.' Francis Pastorious became a very important and influential figure in Philadelphia society boasting the biggest library in the city with an impressive collection of 250 books, mostly theological, in English, Latin, German, Dutch and French. He was also a prolific author and a compiler who filled fifty manuscript volumes with chronicles, collections of moral sayings, poetry and pedagogical exercises composed in several languages. He was deeply respected in the upper echelons of Philadelphian Society while remaining humble and admired by the new immigrant German Quakers and although he continued to be a non-practicing Quaker himself he was accepted and acknowledged by the group and became a teacher in their schools and a leader of their community. Others who came into contact with him probably believed he was destined for great things in the new country. With the weight of his many accomplishments it is even more to his credit when we discover his highly developed moral code was ahead of his time, - by a couple of centuries! In 1688 he led the first public protest against slavery in America, an amazing and humbling thought!

There is a monument to Pastorius which is important enough for me to include some of the sentiments written, so amazed and impressed by the life and work of a man I had not met until today. "Nearly 300 years ago, four men joined to write a strong statement against human injustice. All were members of the religious group called the Society of Friends, or Quakers. On April 28th, 1688 they gathered to address the issue of slavery. Slavery contradicted the Golden Rule. White men had no right to enslave black African men and women. Pastorius continued - people had 'liberty of conscience.' Then he asked the crucial and all- important question, "all new immigrants to this land had come to escape oppression, how could they now, with that conscience, take on the role of the oppressors?"

The Morris Arboretum which was an impressive ninety-two acre Victorian landscape garden of winding paths, streams, large flower beds and a lovely rose garden all run by the University of Pennsylvania, was close by. Also on the main road, the original cobble- stoned thoroughfare called Germantown Avenue, stood the Woodmere Art Museum, another nineteenth-century architectural gem. Its' focus was on showing the work of local artists from the larger Philadelphia region, showing a respectable collection of historical and contemporary art. Most of these new discoveries were all within reasonable walking distance, but one special treasure was only five minutes from our little attic retreat, you could practically smell its freshly cut grass. Around the corner stood the handsome Philadelphia Cricket Club – yes, that most English of English games - CRICKET – not a game associated with Americans, but the players, true to English tradition, even wore 'all whites!' There was also superb, tournament quality grass, lovingly cared for, both for cricket and for the tennis courts. Sitting proudly on this site was a large, handsome 19th century club house, oozing period character and the whole area boasted flower beds and luscious green grass which my father would have admired enormously. He would have more than admired the inviting landmark, he would have loved it enough to taken up immediate residence in Chestnut Hill! Just adjacent to the club was an old and adorable little church with an unusual name for an American church. It was named after the landmark church in London originally built in 1222 and the site of St Martin's since Norman times. 'Saint Martin in the Fields' named after the lovely London church which was originally set in the middle of fields on what was then the outskirts of the city.

Naturally as London grew rapidly in population over the centuries those 'fields' were needed for the city's bewildering growth, and an array of other structures and styles and thoroughfare's and the hundreds of square miles of open country became the bedrock for London's vast expansion and the city we know today. The layout for the infrastructure we now recognize, basically grew out of those 'fields' which is why hundreds of years later the lovely church ended up being, not in the center of the fields, but surrounded and almost in the center of the throbbing city that was built around the church and now sits very close to the bustle of Trafalgar Square where millions of people and pigeons walk or fly past it every day. Now I was living within the shadow of its name sake in the Pennsylvanian town of Chestnut Hill six miles from Philadelphia.

It was all very pretty and a great place to explore. We discovered that Chestnut Hill was fortunate to be nestled along the 1,800 acres of the Wissahickon Valley Park, part of Philadelphia's 9,200 acre Fairmount Park, the emerald necklace and the largest city park in the country. This lovely, wooded valley had the Wissahickon Creek running through its entire seven mile length. The name 'Wissahickon' was a Native American name from the Lenape Indians and the translation meant 'stream of yellowish colour' or 'catfish creek.' We lived close enough to walk down the very steep path to the park from our home and once over the old, still handsome stone bridge we were delighted to find the fast moving, bubbling creek to be quite wide in places and deep enough for a canoe and the agreeable home to families of ducks and geese It was also home to the quaint and charming old Valley Green Inn which served a good lunch and dinner in this lovely natural environment. Legend places the Inn back to British ownership as early as 1683 and the present Inn may indeed incorporate some parts of the original, earlier structure although its existence as a fully functioning Inn probably did not begin until the 1850's when there was access to a sturdy road. We also know that William Penn purchased part of a one hundred acre tract of land including the existing structure there in 1685. In any event, the park today provides residents and visitors alike with delightful access to walking, jogging, biking, horseback riding, picnicking and fishing and we made frequent use of this charming all-year round facility on our doorstep on a weekly basis.

In the mid- 1800's there were many reasons for the affluent to move from the inner city to Chestnut Hill. One of the reasons prosperous Philadelphians fled the city was to escape the summer heat of the low-lying, old city – as I had did! Before their large, handsome houses were built and ready to occupy people probably stayed at the Chestnut Hill Hotel on Germantown Avenue which had been an Inn since 1772 and was rebuilt in 1865 and still operates as a hotel with a decent restaurant and bar. We gravitated to this cozy venue, full of old character and it was where we found one of the best bars and food and a welcoming ambience which was conveniently within walking distance from our own snug little resting place. In his definitive history Prof. David Contosta's book "Suburb in the City: Chestnut Hill" mentions the importance of the railroad link provided in 1854, which allowed for suburban development to take off leading to the building of three separate commuter train stations all within approximately two miles of each other in what was now a thriving town. The new town grew and prospered as they provided services to the new suburbanites and the new commuters, who for their part depended on the city of Philadelphia for their livelihood and culture.

    I was slowly settling in and exploring the environs of my latest home, but I was still planning to fulfill my determined desire to drive to Washington once a week for rehearsals at the Cathedral and looked forward to the final concert of the wonderful Missa Solemnis. The city was calling me and good old friends were awaiting my arrival in favorite, pre-arranged lunch venues about the city and I also intended to squeeze in a few gallery exhibits while I was there. I was excited and anxious to get on the road again. I really enjoyed the long three hour drive, in both directions, sometimes I drove for hours alone with my thoughts, sometimes with the company of music, but never once did I feel unsure of my decision to continue, stealing this extra year to sing with the National Cathedral Chorus. I felt a spring in my step and looked forward to the experience all week and with a sense of freedom and accomplishment as I drove south to the capitol. Reilly could always be relied upon to select choral pieces which were both challenging and also relevant but he was also aware that at the end of the year he would be handing his chorus over to Maestro Shaw to perform Beethoven's masterpiece.

As the Cathedral's resident conductor, preparing his singers for the big event held extra responsibility for him as some of the 'glory' would also be shared by him. We had performed a number of concerts over the preceding months and were well warmed up vocally and emotionally as he worked with us on the note reading and all the other preliminary necessities so that when Maestro Shaw arrived we would be ready for him to work on the fine details and mold us to the exact desires of his interpretation of the work. – we all wanted to shine and dedicated ourselves to making the event unforgettable for all concerned and everyone's mind was focused and counting down the weeks before we would be with Maestro Shaw when we could begin rehearsing and studying Beethoven's great score, the Missa Solemnis. Having finally arrived from my weekly journey I walked up the steps to the Cathedral and through the heavy, familiar and welcoming great doors into the dim light of the nave. It was always a surprise how much pleasure it was to be in that space and how immediately it affected me. Looking all around, I then slowly walked, enjoying all the familiar pleasures of the place while making my way gradually towards our rehearsal space and the early groups of chorus singers standing in clusters quietly chatting, exchanging smiles and greetings, assembling for the evening's rehearsal, finding their places, taking some quiet time before the rehearsal began to rid the mind of the days chores and settle quietly within themselves, preparing mentally and physically for the task ahead. Well on time, everyone was in their place waiting for Reilly to bounce his way to the rostrum, a grin on his lips and a baton in his hand ready for the down beat for our last rehearsal with him before the big man from Atlanta arrived to take over.

Why all the fuss? Simply put, the two great men, Beethoven

and Shaw were giants among men each for their great individual talent, and in their coming together in this concert they were a wonderful match for each other. Their talents were simpatico. The most revered and complex composer of all time is Ludwig Van Beethoven. His music conveys his pain, and his ability to live with, overcome and rise beyond that pain and to share his humanity and compassion with all people. He considered the Missa Solemnis his greatest work, his Masterpiece, the work intended to stand 'outside of time.' It is very difficult and puts huge technical demands on all the musicians, especially the singers. Robert Shaw, whose mind and spirit could carry out Beethoven's demands also understood that pain, he was sensitive to human anguish all his life and the gift of his musical genius was to take the most detailed and sensitive nuances in choral music and convey it gently but powerfully to a large group of singers who with his direction and their voices would then connect these human emotions to the audience. Robert Shaw left an unsurpassed, worldwide legacy of excellence in his interpretation of all the choral music, written through the ages.

For reasons unknown to me we did not use our usual rehearsal space inside the Cathedral but one located in a small building which was part of the Cathedral real estate and usually used for the boy choristers rehearsal, so the space was very intimate. When we had found our comfort level in the smaller space I felt it was an even better place to rehearse this piece than the cavernous Cathedral itself. If we could get it right in this small space no detail would be missed in the large Cathedral or at the Kennedy Centre, both venues seating at least 2,000 adoring fans of this work. Robert Shaw was within touching distance of all of us and he could listen in detail to our individual voices. His presence was inspiring in itself. He frequently stopped the rehearsal to express his interpretation of a particular measure, phrase or text, emphasizing the precise sound and dynamic he required, the exact pronunciation and emotion he wanted to hear from each individual and voice section, but more intensely, the honest depth of feeling that we could collectively produce and connect to the listeners. It was very intense. Our eyes were glued on him, his baton and on our score. But we occasionally dared to take a second to scribble in furious shorthand into the margin of the score, so as to remember his words and savor the gems that dropped continuously from his lips before he quickly moved on to emphasize again what he wanted from us. He also explained why the next phrase was important, or why a particular note illuminated the phrase, and why it was important for him to share the story with us, about the music itself, about Beethoven the man and Beethoven the composer. In his passion he also stressed the individual responsibility of our own group of singers whose job it was to convey all this to the audience - the text, and the musical magnificence of this masterpiece. If you could keep up with his pace, the experience was wildly exhilarating!

As a group, however, we began to observe worrying signs regarding the Maestro's health, he appeared much older and he had recently been ill and we could see he had more than the usual passion about him, it was more an air of determination. But we were also immersed all the while in the deep concentration required of us by the Maestro, little else in our lives existed – we moved as if in a trance – we lived in an other-worldly place during our exposure to Robert Shaw, Ludwig Van Beethoven and what the two of them expected of us and for which we each individually had to reach deep down inside ourselves to find and deliver

Robert Shaw was very popular and a huge draw for the public and the first concert in the cathedral was sold out months in advance and judging from the reviews the performance was a huge success for all concerned. The second concert at the Kennedy Centre was welcomed and applauded by another full house. No one in that audience knew, however, that the second concert nearly didn't take place. All chorus performers and musicians were in place and on the Kennedy Centre stage waiting for our Maestro, but he didn't appear! A reasonable delay became an unusual and long delay which gave way to worried whispers that soon became loud murmurs and mumbles of deep concern that something serious had happened to our Maestro, our Leader. Up to the podium leapt an unfamiliar gentleman who arrived with apologies and reassurances but with a worried expression on his face, introducing himself as Mr. Shaw's Assistant Conductor who would take the orchestral and choral dress rehearsal himself and announcing that Mr. Shaw was unwell and resting in his hotel. He had brought a message from the Maestro to the assembled company that we were not to worry, that he would be just fine for the performance the following day! But we were all very worried knowing that his health had been a concern for a while and that the demands in terms of time and emotion and sheer energy could be a challenge for an eighty year old man with a heart condition. All the participants sang and played with some reserve during the rehearsal, everyone worrying about Maestro Shaw, and while we pondered the possibility that he might not be well enough to conduct the concert we remained positive and mutually decided that we would make it a magnificent performance of the Missa Solemnis, one for Mr. Shaw to be proud of and for all the singers and performers to remember for the rest of their lives.

Conserving his energy during the warm up before the performance the following day, he stopped the orchestra and chorus and with a wry, worn smile he found a few amusing words to reassure us, - except that they didn't! The words were supposed to make us smile but they were a little strange and ended up making us feel nervous. His words to this effect were - "Don't worry if I keel over, just carry on and keep the beat in time to my pacemaker!" Was he was serious? We did all make it through the performance and it was the amazing musical event everyone

MARY NEVILLE

expected. However, it did sadly become his last performance and in less than two months later Robert Shaw had a massive stroke and died in New Haven, Connecticut at the age of 82 years. And the world of music mourned.

During our period of mourning for Robert Shaw, I found a web site called 'Chorus America', and a page where choristers share their most memorable experiences. Under 'Memorable Conductors' there is a comment which uses a word which described the whole experience. – "Singing the Missa Solemnis with Robert Shaw at the Kennedy Center in one of the last major concerts he conducted, the Maestro had been very unwell and missed the dress rehearsal. But when he came to conduct the concert, the chorus was completely connected as a group and the experience was totally transcendent." Yes, it was indeed transcendent!

My year away had been deeply memorable and that in deciding to drive to Washington to participate in a great experience I knew I had been correct to listen to my inner voice. I sometimes struggled not to be over- ruled by events beyond my control, and relied on my inner voice which was always there and always to be trusted. I listened again to that faithful voice - and that was how I also knew that I would not join another choral group, however tempting the music or famous the group. I wanted the experience I had had in the lovely city of Washington, with my friends and fellow singers and the much-applauded, life- changing, and deeply memorable job we had shared together, was inspired by many things. The two beautiful venues, the great composer and his music, the great conductor and his inspiration and the thousands in the audiences who came to share the experience and who were visibly moved and uplifted by it, these would remain among my most treasured memories. I could not imagine being able to be that close to such a truly transcendent experience ever again.

With Beth's return to the United States and the city of Philadelphia after more than a decades' absence while she was living out of the country, either studying in Montreal or pursuing more studies and her future employment in London, my dear daughter was now close by - we were both in the same city. She was excited to be back in the US. She had successfully finished her post doctorate in Cardiff, Wales - a beautiful part of Britain which unfortunately has little sun and lots of rain, and so the soft sunny light and warm, hot and clammy climate in Philadelphia was a pleasure which agreed with her enormously. So did the city itself. So did her new husband. So did her job at the University of Pennsylvania where her goal was a happy and determinedly challenging one – quite simply she wanted to cure blindness, among other things! She was not in any way daunted by the prospect of setting such a high goal for herself, after all she had always set high goals for herself and overcome many trials, so I didn't doubt for a moment that she would succeed in her efforts. I also like to think that the fact that her mother and father now lived only a short distance away and were always delighted to be invited to share some of her first friends and new experiences, made her return all the richer.

Andrew would remain in his job in Washington for several more years and although he was reasonably close, just a three hour drive away, I still missed him very much and I continued to be grateful to him for his hospitality and support during my weekly journeys to DC for the year I call The Robert Shaw Year. Andrew had made a good life for himself in the nations' capitol and had lots of friends and had found interesting and useful employment allowing him to remain independent while he gained great experience in the area of corporate fund raising. This made it easy when he did return to quickly find a good fit for his skills and talents in Philadelphia and within a few weeks he had himself set up in an apartment in the city which he really enjoyed. Still not finding the need to own a car he explored every inch of his new city on foot and mastered the public transport system when necessary like a native. In many ways he preferred Philadelphia to Washington because it had more depth and he appreciated its 'real people' and its history and the architecture that complemented it. Andrew also had a ready-made set of new friends, thanks to his sister and brother- in- law who already knew a wide circle of people, some of whom were also great characters.

With Andrew's return to Philadelphia, his happy presence completed our family's small circle. After all the many addresses and wanderings we had individually experienced since we were last here together, our reunion in this first American city where we had arrived with our few belongings in May 1968, brought all of us back to the place we started from. Turn, turn! I felt it brought a broader understanding of the family having 'come full circle'. We had each lived in many towns, cities and states and countries, and now we had all individually experienced what it meant to end where we had started, in the first city, and first home and we hoped, our final destination in the United States of America. We had all travelled far. Our individual and collective experiences could not yet be compared with the words in T.S. Eliot's poem entitled 'Little Gidding' which will come later, but the line 'Will be to arrive where we first started' does fit. And it did feel like a series of circles within circles and while I was probably the only one that still hoped that we would eventually arrive back on to English soil and that the 'three- thousand- mile- full- circle' was still possible, I realized I was probably out- numbered in that hope, and it wasn't going to happen unless I journeyed alone. Although it was not complete in that respect, it was at this point, still a comforting closure for all of us.

For both Andrew and Beth the city was a good balance of size and conveniences coupled with history, architecture and the arts and there were lots of new people to befriend, good things to discover and rediscover, and open spaces to explore and enjoy. Its' proximity to New York City and the regular train service provided from Philadelphia was another large plus. It had also grown in a good way in our absence – there had been much expansion and elegant skyscrapers gave the sky line an interesting prospect and there was more sophistication and choice among the interesting modern shops and enticing restaurants. There was a new Visitors Centre and the buildings of Old City around the lovely Independence Hall area were well maintained and manicured giving Philadelphia its rightful dignity and pride of place as the nation's first city. Beth and Andrew immediately began looking up their old friends from early days in Pennsylvania and across the river in New Jersey, all of whom brought them that sense of the continuing thread, those natural needs of re-connecting with the past which are very necessary for every individual and something which I have continued to do with my old friends and relatives in England since the beginning.

The brood was together again. For many years I had yearned for us all to be together as a family and so there was much rejoicing and genuine happiness. For all of us to 'come home' to the same city at almost the same time was an unusual coincidence. This happy, comfortable and convenient coming together of families doesn't easily or necessarily happen in this wide open continent of a country where there are many different reasons for people to move.

The immensity of the land in America allows people to explore just because they can – they are exercising their right for what America stands for - it is often simply called, Freedom! Although other circumstances may intervene citizens do have the intrinsic understanding that they really are free to live anywhere regardless of their color, creed or the many former obstacles of their past lives, and if they don't like it where they find themselves then they are free to explore the immensity of the land and the complexities of its culture knowing it belongs to them and is there to embrace.

Throughout this book, with genuine interest and desire, I have embraced America and tried to understand its history and multitude of customs and the different aspects of life in a country that has so many wide open spaces and so many opportunities for people. A country where everybody who arrives on it shores comes originally from somewhere else but has agreed to embrace a new land and to collectively learn a new language and enjoy all that a fresh beginning offers. I arrived as a very reluctant immigrant but as I look back on my years in America I have had so many benefits and my new life here has been rich in experiences and both interesting and personally rewarding. For my own understanding I have continuously attempted to make honest comparisons between the two cultures, linked closely as they are by blood and history.

In this process I finally realized what I missed most about the country I left behind, England. It was the nation's collective knowledge of its two thousand year history and the visual awareness of that ancient history which can be seen everywhere, scattered across the land. There are many examples of the early 'invaders' of Britain and architectural ruins and relics cover over the entire country.

You could say that since the Romans, Britain's long list of invader's wanted the place so much that they fought among themselves for centuries to control the land they had discovered and loved. They brought with them their high ranking nobles who divided the land between them and organized it into villages and small towns with neat county borders. They eventually stopped fighting and farmed the land and became law abiding citizens with strict but sensible rules and laws which all citizens had to respect, or suffer the consequences! Gradually they melted and mingled, as did most of the other invaders into the general population giving us a rich and merry mix of language, heritage and history. Britain is like a living museum. There are countless examples of the early 'invaders' of Britain and architectural ruins and relics abound across the entire land and are found in villages, towns and cities where our ancient ancestry becomes an open book. Castles, churches, cathedrals, palaces, abbeys and forts still stand, dotted across the landscape, some teetering on the edge of wet windy headlands or nestling in the soft cradle of the Green Man's forest, many, many of them now, just ghostly ruins.

In writing this I often adopted the role of Janus, the Roman God of 'transitions and beginnings' or 'past and future' and who is depicted as having two faces, both looking at the same time in opposite directions, always making comparisons, perhaps weighing the two visions side by side, trying honestly to be fair to each image. A person or object that is 'Janus faced' has two contrasting aspects. And I have reached a place of peace within myself, loving and respecting both visions as I acknowledge, accept and celebrate the many differences and similarities that will always exist between the two nations where I have lived my life.

The English - American Thomas Paine who was born in Norfolk, England in 1737 and emigrated to 'the new world' in 1774 became one of the most respected men of that enlightened period and is considered to be the thinker and writer who penned the words that closely resemble a phrase that has made a long journey in time and has been delivered to us in its modified form and now finds itself in common usage. I will now rest my pen with these words - 'The world is my country, and mankind my race.'

MARY NEVILLE

My Family's New Americans

Julian Mitchell Clark was born in Philadelphia January 4th 2000
Sophie Patricia Clark was born in Philadelphia August 19th 2003

Little Gidding

A people without history
Is not redeemed from time, for history is a pattern
Of timeless moments. So, while the light fails
On a winter's afternoon, in a secluded chapel
History is now and England.

We shall not cease from exploration
And the end of all our exploring
Will be to arrive where we started
And know the place for the first time.

—an excerpt from *Four Quartets* by T. S. Eliot

On Westminster Bridge

Earth hath not anything to show more fair,
Dull would he be of sight who could pass by
A sight so touching in its majesty,
This city now doth, like a garment wear
The beauty of the morning, silent, bare,
Ships, towers, domes, theatres and temples lie
Open unto the fields and to the sky,
All bright and glittering in the smokeless air.
Never did sun more beautifully steep
In its first splendor, valley, rock or hill,
Ne'er saw I, never felt, a calm so deep!
This river glideth at his own sweet will,
Dear God! The very houses seem asleep
And all that mighty heart is lying still.

— William Wordsworth

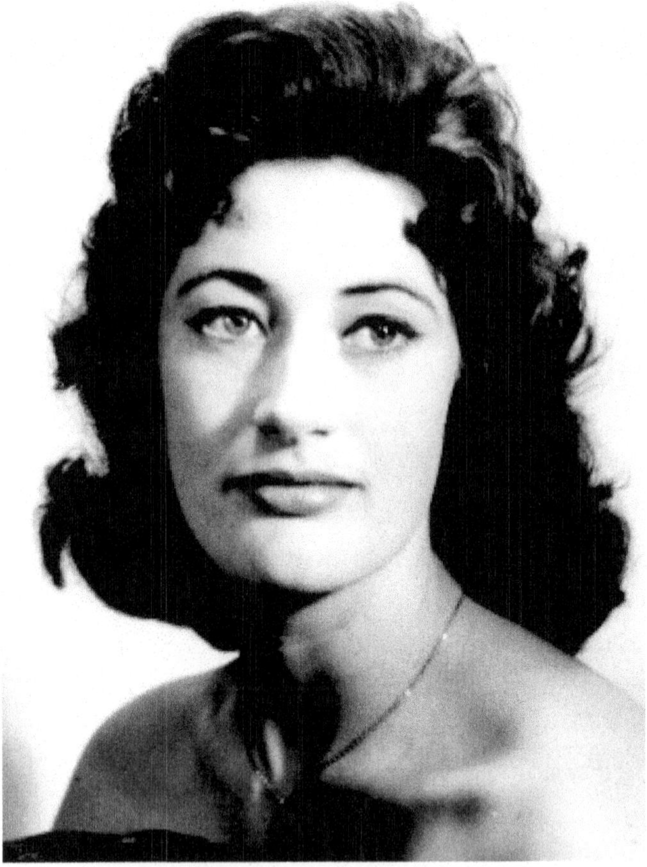

About the Author

American corporations were expanding in the sixties and looking to employ highly qualified talent to fill new jobs, turning to England and Western Europe to pursue young men with a PhD in the sciences. This influx of bright, new and highly qualified talent was generally referred to as The Brain Drain. An invitation came as a happy surprise to the male member of the Neville family who had recently acquired the qualification in physics which he had worked hard for and deserved. He was just what the generous corporation in America needed and the invitation to join the company sounded like a dream come true. But the news came as an unpleasant surprise to his spouse. Having just moved into a newly built and newly furnished home in London she intended to stay put with her new baby and his three year old sister. To leave London for a place called Philadelphia was unthinkable. She couldn't imagine leaving the great ancient city, the city of her birth, and was proud of being a Londoner. She knew every street and every park and was thrilled as she walked beside the lovely old homes, many bearing the prestigious blue plaque signifying the contribution made to the city by famous Londoners - writers, dramatists, actors, musicians, poets and artists, their history going back many hundreds of years. She loved all the old theatres and concert halls, pubs, museums, cobble stoned alley ways, the bridges over the great River Thames and she intended to share the joys of London with her children. Why should she leave it all? The story describes her challenging adjustment but gradual and sincere acceptance and respect for America. She wanted to understand the history in the seven states she lived, and takes time peeling back the individual layers revealing not only the well- known historical events but also many unusual connections to England not generally known. She began to embrace and respect America by delving deeply into the country's history, and this led to her happily becoming a citizen in the country that became her new home. This being achieved it allowed her to freely embrace her own successful musical career and enjoy other surprising and exciting developments, especially one that occurred while living in the nation's capital and which added to her continuing respect and pleasure in America.